SACRED SHADOW, SACRED GROUND

A Vietnam War Widow's Journey Through Unresolved Grief

Glenda M. Carter

Two Rainbows Publishing
North Powder, Oregon

Copyright © 2004 by Glenda M. Carter

All rights reserved. No part of this publication may be reproduced, stored in a retrieval system or transmitted in any form or by any means, electronic, mechanical, photocopying, recording or otherwise, without written permission of the publisher.

Carter, Glenda M.
Sacred Shadow, Sacred Ground: A Vietnam War Widow's Journey Through Unresolved Grief

Library of Congress Control Number 2004098
ISBN 0-9762289-0-4

Book Design/Layout: Bushwhack Graphics; Glenda Carter
Cover Design Consultation: Jim Carney
Cover Photo: Glenda Carter
Editors: Rosina Armon; Lisa Britton; Timothy Lucas
Printed by Color Press, Walla Walla, Wash.
Manufactured in the United States of America

First Edition, November 2004

Two Rainbows Publishing
PO Box 89
North Powder, OR 97867

www.tworainbowspublishing.com
order@tworainbowspublishing.com

For Lisa, Sherry, Imogene,
Douglas, Morgan, Rhonda,
Jake, Justin, Zanette, Crystal
and Zachary

God's Peace
Glenda M. Carter

Contents

Page	Section
1	Introduction
7	Beginning My Journey
15	We Regret to Inform You
43	Through the Valley of Grief and Losses
64	Boys to Men, a poem
65	Ambushed
73	Ambushed Near Liberty Bridge
85	Missing Links, a poem
93	The Seven
119	Welcome Home
129	It Was an Epiphany, a poem
131	It's You, It's Me, a poem
133	Photographs: Vietnam Veterans Memorial
147	Lost Child
151	Memorial Day
159	Finale
167	Good-Bye Letters
175	Afterword: "It Is Finished"
179	Acknowledgments
186	Recommended Reading
187	About the Author

INTRODUCTION

Sacred Shadow, Sacred Ground

This brave and beautiful book affirms something I have long believed: the flag on the coffin covers only the obvious tragedy.

Every bullet, bomb, land mine, mortar round or grenade that killed an American soldier in Vietnam stopped other lives here dead in their tracks.

The life Glenda Carter thought she was going to lead and the future she thought she was going to live ended, exactly three months after she was married, on September 14, 1968 when, as she puts it, "the Vietnam war came to my doorstep," with the unbearable news that it would take her 36 years to heal; her husband, Bruce Carter, was dead, killed by a bullet to his head on September 11, 1968.

Glenda Carter had never seen her Marine husband in his dress blues until she looked at him in his coffin. There was no face to see for the last time, no cold cheek to kiss. His head was swaddled in bandages. For decades her soul would be bound and hidden away from a world that truth be told— cared very little for women like Glenda.

Go on, get over it, you'll be married again one day said the man who tried to talk Glenda out of buying a burial plot next to her husband. His crude, blunt honesty is why so many never heal. Grief is dismissed, diminished and discounted in our culture as if it's just something to "get over" like a small step or a high curb.

For years, Glenda Carter felt as though she was "on a raft,

Introduction (cont'd)

drifting around a cesspool."

Her husband was dead. But her love for him was not. "When you died, I lost not only you, I lost me," and her heart was held hostage for years and years and years.

She was, for a time, able to put on a happy-go-lucky face. She got degrees and held jobs. She became a passionate photographer.

And then she came undone. There was depression, despair and suicide attempts. When people asked what she did for a living, she wanted to say, "I spend my time doing what it takes to survive."

And yet, and yet, you're holding this book in your hands. Something happened. Although at times they may have been no more than a blink apart, Glenda Carter's will to live was stronger than her desire to die.

The writer Annie Dillard once wrote, in effect, "that pain is a terrible thing to waste." Glenda Carter has not wasted an ounce of her grief or an atom of her agony.

She has wrestled with her dark demons and marched through those moments she never thought she could.

Healing, ultimately, is a gift that comes through grace. Glenda felt the steadfast support of therapists she turned to and she felt God's presence alongside her in her perilous journey through grief. She, like veterans, had PTSD. Her trauma was combat-related. While it didn't happen in Vietnam, it happened because of Vietnam. And for Glenda, as for so may veterans, "the only way over was through."

In the end, she experienced slightly more than a decade of grief for each month of her three-month marriage as Mrs. Bruce L. Carter. But now, something beautiful has been born

Sacred Shadow, Sacred Ground

from Bruce and Glenda's love. This is a book of healing, and ultimately, a book of hope and finally, courage.

We are never more courageous than when we dare to love. Rarely do we even catch a whiff of just how vulnerable we are when we love another as much, or more, than we love ourselves.

And yet, there is a love that bombs can't shatter and bullets can't kill. Our lives are mysteries wrapped in paradox. As Glenda separates herself from her sadness, she feels closer to Bruce than ever before.

By the end of *Sacred Shadow, Sacred Ground*, Glenda Carter has done more than negotiate a cease-fire with her self. She has found peace, which is always so much more than just the absence of war.

At times, healing is a lonely and treacherous journey. But what emerges from Glenda's saga is the reminder that what is loneliest of all is to live a life barren of love.

Letting go is never easy and the outcome never sure but Glenda's life was so blessed by Bruce's abundant love, that in the end, there was some for you and me.

You are holding their love in your hands. Take it, use it, give it away. In this barren and beleaguered world there is always someone at our very fingertips whose life can shine more brightly through our love.

Laura Palmer

Laura Palmer

Laura Palmer was a reporter in Vietnam from 1972–1974. She is the author of *Shrapnel in the Heart* and has also written about Vietnam in *War Torn*.

Walden

"...I went to the woods because I wished to live deliberately, to front only the essential facts of life, and see if I could not learn what it had to teach, and not, when I come to die, discover that I had not lived."

—Henry David Thoreau

Glenda & Bruce, 1968

BEGINNING MY JOURNEY

Sacred Shadow, Sacred Ground

For 33 years I kept the dilapidated cardboard box the military sent to me after Bruce was killed in Vietnam. It contained personal items of clothing, his dog tags, letters I wrote to him, the Bible I gave him for his 18th birthday, his wedding ring and his Zodiac watch that looked like it had been shot off his arm. Other numerous items included the silver necklace he wore with St. Christopher on one side and the Marine insignia on the other. It was the one we placed between our lips as we kissed good-bye.

These items confirmed that Bruce was dead.

For a long time I left the withering container unattended in the basement of my parents' home. Sometimes I would quietly slip away and go down the narrow wooden steps that led to the unfinished room where Bruce's last belongings sat hidden away among other discarded treasures. I thought about the first time I saw him. He had finished basic training. His light brown hair was acquiring length and the pipe he smoked indicated a deeper maturity than did the teenage whiskers on his face. I held his things to my heart and cried the tears of a lost young girl.

The single light bulb hanging from the bare wooden rafters in the center of the room was the only electrical light source. The gray cement walls and floor kept the room cool and dark.

The dampness and musty smell signaled that no one

actually lived in this part of the house.

In the early 1970's the most horrible reality slapped me in the face. While holding the light green shirt he wore after our wedding I awoke to the fact that Bruce was not ever going to come home. No matter how many tears I shed or how hard I prayed, my sweet Bruce would never be back. More of my heart died that day. As the finality of death made it's appearance, I took another dip into the hollow darkness and advanced further into the shadows of despair. My wounded self continued to roam more desperately, searching for a reason to live and a place to belong.

In the 1980's I periodically tried to convince myself that I was "letting go" and began to give his things away. I started moving the remainder of his possessions with me, keeping the bulky box near but out of sight.

In 1991 I was looking for reasons my life continued to crumble even after my greatest efforts to find peace and happiness. My subconscious must have been trying to tell me the answer all along. The sacred memories locked in my heart stirred as my weary body sit next to the worn-down box on the '60's orange, shag carpet in my bedroom.

My tears dripped onto the pages as I relived the words I wrote to Bruce. Then, one by one I placed the letters onto the flames in the wood stove.

I thought that by getting rid of the letters I wrote to Bruce, it would also destroy any proof or written history of my feelings. The testament of my love for him would go up in smoke and disappear like he did. I could avoid having to confront the complexity of the loss of my youth. I would not ever have to relive my thoughts, dreams and hopes of the springtime of my life.

As I burned memories of myself, my journey toward self-destruction continued to spiral downward.

Thank God I did not burn the letters Bruce had written to me.

In 2001, I emotionally, physically and financially hit bottom. The accumulation of lost jobs, relationships and my health overwhelmed me. In the past, I was able to pick myself up and approach life with some facility of "normal." When I wasn't able to hold myself together, I would just move on to another job, another person, another town, and continue to build on the life of my false self. But this time was different. I was not able to bounce back. My survival skills were worn out and used up.

Often I would find myself sitting on the couch staring out the window and suddenly realize I had been there for hours. I was grossly overweight. My five-foot frame topped out at 248 pounds.

I was in serious emotional, physical and financial trouble.

When my faith started to grow weary I knew it was time to make a change. I believe I was allowed to exhaust all my former dreams and ambitions so I could let go of my self-serving desires and confidently move into the will of God, knowing that I had tried everything possible.

Even so, I fought hard to keep from surrendering my will. I came to understand the meaning of the words in the song, "Me and Bobby McGee": "Freedom's just another word for nothing left to lose..."

Beginning My Journey

The crossroads of my life insisted that I make a choice. My "I can do it all alone" attitude had to go. I was beaten. It was very humbling to turn my will over and choose life over death. I began to pray more frequently. At night I visualized placing myself into the comforting arms of God and allowed God to comfort me. In the middle of my life transition, I began to feel a sense of peace.

I was very thankful when my property sold for just enough money to pay my bills and allow me to move to be closer to family. It was painful to let go of my past and all the things I worked so hard to keep, but the more I let go the better I began to feel.

Moving from my dream place with three bedrooms and two baths on a two-acre mini-farm, to a small, one-bedroom rental was a challenge. I was close to the mountain and called my new place "The cabin." There was still snow on the ground. The cold weather chilled me to the core.

For several days I had no *Internet* service or even a television to watch. The door of my mind began to open and I cried for my most recent losses. I thought I was making new discoveries about heartache, only to hear the words come back at me from the local Country & Western radio station. There had been a song written about everything I was feeling. Every new concept in my awakening brain had already been felt, written and sung about. I was not the first, nor would I be the last, to have a broken heart. I would live, though I felt as if I would die.

This move convinced me that all the excess baggage from my past lives had to go, including my emotional baggage. There was no place for storage, no money to rent a storage unit and no energy to pack and unpack "things." There it was, waiting in the center of my bantam living room, demanding my immediate attention. With its silent voice the 1968 cardboard box from Vietnam once again beckoned my heart to explore its contents.

I decided I would read Bruce's letters one last time, then place them into a smaller box and never, ever open it again.

The mere thought of saying good-bye to Bruce caused my heart to feel shattered. I held his watch and sobbed uncontrollably. Through my tears I saw the scratched face of the 33-year-old Zodiac watch. It began to tick. I visualized a serious look on Bruce's face and could see the concerned expression in his blue eyes as if he were pleading with me to listen.

It is time.

I knew exactly what that meant. The time had come for me to choose to deal with the loss of Bruce, or not.

It was as if I had touched the root of buried grief that entangled my soul. I recognized that this chain of events had brought me onto the stage of opportunity. I continued to cry. The emotional pain was intense as I held his watch against my chest and accepted the call to begin the journey that would free my tormented soul from the grasp of my unresolved grief.

Beginning My Journey

We Regret to Inform You...

Sacred Shadow, Sacred Ground

In March of 2001 my therapist suggested I look on the World Wide Web and try to find other women who lost their husbands in the Vietnam War. This would be the beginning of my pursuit for resolution. After typing the words "war widow" into a search engine text box on the browser window of my computer, the magic of the *Internet* took me to a website called "Widows of War Living Memorial."

The site, inspired by the 1998 documentary film, "Regret to Inform," provides a forum for widows of all wars to share their stories. The accounts of loss were pointed and brief. The website had not been in existence long at that time; most entries were written in 2000 and 2001.

I struggled to read the stories that sounded all too familiar. As they triggered my emotions, I felt myself become antsy and irritable. I forced myself to continue because finally, after 30 years, I found a connection that made me feel less alone.

My subconscious grasped onto the words, "Regret to Inform," and wouldn't let go.

A couple of the women mentioned how they felt when they first heard the familiar phrase. My own thoughts leaped back to 1968 when two Marine officers sat across from my mother and me and said, "We regret to inform you..."

We Regret to Inform You...

As I read these other widows' stories, I tried to recall my own but came up against a mental fog. However, I knew by my emotional and physical response to the words "Regret to Inform" that it was time to wake up and dig up those memories, embrace the pain and resolve the grief. Yet, I still did not have a clear understanding of how those words had been affecting my life.

The "Regret to Inform" link led me to the site of the documentary film about widows of the Vietnamese-American War. After reading about it I tried to order the film but was unable to get a copy. I filled out the order, left my charge card number, but got no response. During the several times I revisited the site, I thought about reordering the film, but for whatever reason never got around to it.

Memories slowly clawed their way to the surface. I diligently wrote about them in my journal and talked about them with my therapist. I learned to help them escape from the darkness, confront them, grieve over them, accept them, and finally, release them.

Nothing in the short history of my life had prepared me for the day the Vietnam War came to my doorstep. I was 19, naive; the war was "over there." Bruce and I had our whole lives ahead of us, and I believed God could and would miraculously protect Bruce in the middle of a war.

During the time Bruce was gone I lived with my parents and continued to work as an aide at the local nursing home where Bruce and I had met. On a small calendar by my bed I wrote down my work hours each night before going to sleep. One night I broke down and cried as an inner voice repeated,
He's dead, Bruce is dead, Oh my God, Bruce is dead.
I told myself, *This is crazy, I'm just being fearful, stop!* I was so upset that I didn't write on the calendar that night but, instead, turned over and went to sleep.

The next morning, the empty feeling stayed with me in spite of the letter I received from Bruce. I wrote more letters back to him trying to get rid of that hollow feeling, though without success. A few days later I went bowling with a school friend to distract myself and fill the emptiness inside.

Dismissing the experience as simply fear just was not working.

On the morning of September 14, the military messenger of death pulled up in front of my parents' home in the form of a drab green vehicle. Suddenly, I was living a scene out of a war movie and a scene experienced by thousands of families across America.

I knew it was bad as soon as I saw it, and my mother's eyes. I retreated to my bedroom leaving my mom to answer the door. My mind screamed, *No God! No! No! No!* as I clutched my stomach to hold in the anguish.

I heard muffled voices, then my mother calling me into the living room. There was nowhere to run. I had to

We Regret to Inform You

compose myself and hear what they had to say. My heart knew what they were going to say, but I was struggling to maintain hope.

No, it can't be, Bruce can't be dead.

To pull myself together I had to surrender hope and accept defeat. It took all the strength I had to open my bedroom door. Reluctantly, numbly, I walked the hallway to the living room and greeted the two Marines. Later my mother told me it seemed to her like it took me a long time to come out of my room.

One of the two Marines asked us to sit down.

My mother and I sat side by side on our pink couch, while they sat across from us on the black couch. As they began to talk I was hoping against all odds that they would say something other than, "Bruce is dead."

However, I heard them clearly say, "We regret to inform you..."

From then on, everything became a fog. I was in shock and denial. They had to have made a mistake, it wasn't Bruce, it had to have been someone else. There was a mix-up in identity. How could they be sure it was Bruce?

I sat quietly, holding back tears or any expression of emotion; what I felt was anything but quiet. I was torn inside. I didn't understand why God let him die; I knew God could do anything, but why did he let him die?

I pretended to understand what they were saying, but their words did not connect in my mind. Struggling to focus, I felt as if my brain had blown a fuse. I did not cry; crying was a sign of weakness in my family.

It was the '60's, and the whole nation was still grieving

the losses of President John F. Kennedy, Sen. Robert Kennedy and Dr. Martin Luther King Jr., as well as other personal losses resulting from the war. As a young girl I learned, along with many others in our nation, to show my strength by mimicking Jackie Kennedy. I remembered seeing her firmly restrained stance and expressionless veiled face watch as her husband's casket was taken from the rotunda of the Capitol building. She did not let us see the tears of her heart as she walked numbly through the good-bye ceremonies. News commentaries were full of praise for her ability to maintain composure. So, I too, assumed the stance of dignity and strength by not expressing my emotion. We were becoming a desensitized nation.

Although I cannot remember the specifics of the conversation when I felt my mother's hand tighten around mine, I glanced in her direction and could see she was choking back her tears. She later told me that she didn't remember me saying anything except, to tell them I would take care of informing Bruce's sister.

The war that was "over there" somewhere had just come to my front door, into my living room, wounding and taking my heart prisoner, and I didn't shed a tear...then.

Ironically, the Marines later told my brother I took it well. Strange, we cannot see what is inside the heart of another. I felt compassion for them because their job was to bring horrible news to people. I could not cry and lash out at them with my own screams of personal anguish.

My war of survival began that day.

We Regret to Inform You

Soon after they left I struggled with feelings of wanting to die. I thought about running my car into a telephone pole and killing myself. Instead, I chose to live, to accept responsibility for making sure Bruce had a proper burial. I left to tell Bruce's sister while Mom took care of calling my brothers and friends. By the time I returned, it seemed the whole town knew Bruce was dead.

My life was forever altered: within six months, my identity changed from single to married to widow. My sense of direction was destroyed, my inner compass, damaged. I hadn't had a chance to learn how to be a wife—now I'm supposed to be a widow?

Even though Bruce was dead, I still loved him. How would I ever stop? My heart remained married. I didn't know how to be a widow or go back to being single. One does not expect to lose her husband at 19; I refused to call myself a widow.

It took almost two weeks for Bruce's body to be returned home. Meanwhile, I went back to work, which helped me to maintain a connection to what was familiar in my life. One day while standing in the lounge, one of the other aides, who had lost her husband in a vehicle accident, tried to take me under her wing. I looked her straight in the face as she gave me directions to her house and could not comprehend a word she was saying. Even now, I can't remember her name, but I do remember riding with her to her house while she told me about her own loss. In her own way, she was offering me support. She was trying to tell me that we live through these things, but I couldn't accept it at the time. I remember thinking, *I don't want to hear this.*

I found myself avoiding and ignoring people. I could not sit still; I had to stay on the move or people might know how badly I was hurting. I was afraid that if I started crying I wouldn't be able to stop. Within my heart raged a battle between denial and reality.

Scenes of how the funeral would be played in my head. Staying in control meant having no surprises: I could hide my tears.

I cannot recall if it was days, weeks or months before I remembered the premonition about Bruce being killed. When I thought about it, I remembered I stopped writing on my calendar that night. Out of curiosity I found the calendar and discovered it happened the night of September 10, 1968.

It happened between eight and twelve hours prior to Bruce's death. The controversy and unpopularity of the Vietnam War taught us wives and families of soldiers to be silent about our war experiences. I stuffed the words "Regret to Inform" away, along with all the other painful feelings.

My fight to maintain an appearance of sanity continued until 2001.

By late July 2001 I had revisited the start of my personal war, and connected to the words so familiar to

We Regret to Inform You

families of dead soldiers. I picked up a newspaper I don't normally read and was stunned to see the words, "Regret to Inform" in an advertisement. The film would show on August 8, 2001 in Enterprise, Oregon, one day before the 33rd anniversary of when Bruce left the United States for Vietnam. It would be shown in the same town we went to on our brief honeymoon, which was only 80 miles from where I lived at the time.

Enterprise is also where I buried Bruce.

There is no such thing as coincidence; there is, however, a cosmic or divine synchronicity. When I saw the ad, I knew in my heart that God was orchestrating this event. It was one of many similar events I had experienced throughout my recovery process. Because I believed this to be true, I had to go see the film. I could not put it off, ignore it or find an excuse not to go. I had to be there.

It was an "I gotta' go no matter what" feeling.

The war was long over, but I was still wounded and held in emotional captivity. On the one side was all the love and beauty I could dream of, and on the other was all the sorrow and pain imaginable. It felt like two forces going to battle for ownership of my soul and I was in the middle.

Through the process of healing I became familiar with terms like, "slaying the dragons" and dealing with "personal demons." I prepared for a major personal conflict that would open my deepest wound. With a vengeance I was determined to extract the blade from my heart and set myself free.

As I sat facing my therapist, we discussed the issue of

seeing the film. I felt a quiet assurance. In order to be victorious, I had to be willing to walk through dark tunnels and over fiery embers to get to the battlefield.

Emotional wounds are like physical wounds: they must be cleansed and dressed or they can become infected and invite disease. I was tired of being ill. I wanted to pull the dagger from my heart and raise it victoriously in salute to my God.

The highway led me by the winding waters of the Grand Ronde River and into the beautiful valley of the Wallowa Mountains. My mind was making a similar trip in a 1967 blue Rambler 33 years ago after taking Bruce to the airport for the last time. For a moment I was 19 again, full of hope, love, and strength. I walked in confidence then, knowing I was loved and what I wanted in life. My sense of belonging somehow overpowered the sadness of his departure.

The familiarity of the Wallowas began to stir emotions. Since Enterprise represented the best and worst times of my life, I wondered at what point I would feel the painful memories. Needing to gather my thoughts, I pulled over and stopped the car just before rounding the last corner into town.

My greatest fear was that I would not be able to experience the feelings I came to face. I was afraid I would slip into denial or escape into another survival mode.

My eyes burned from lack of sleep the night before. I felt weary. Vacation traffic passed by as I wondered why I was making a big deal about this trip. Other than a general anxiety, I thought I was doing quite well.

Since it was too early to check into the motel, I drove toward the cemetery. Suddenly, I felt nauseated as my car made its way up the narrow incline through the cemetery's front gate.

Sprinkler pipes lay across the road, so I drove toward the dry, empty rolling hills, making the turn at the top that would force me to look at what lay behind.

My God!

Sacred Shadow, Sacred Ground

Before I knew it, I was on the same road Bruce and I walked years ago, facing the same timeless Wallowa Range. The mountains stood before me in their majestic power and glorious beauty, taking my breath and lifting my spirit. I had forgotten how magnificent they were.

As I lay my head back against the seat of my car and closed my tired eyes, I rested knowing I was in a familiar space. For several years after Bruce died this was where I was able to still my troubled mind and allow my memories to surface. I was able to relive the short six months and the few times we spent together from beginning to end. I was able to scale the walls of darkness and experience peace and comfort. However, my memory failed me on this occasion.

A feeling of sadness cloaked me as I realized I couldn't relive our entire life together anymore. A truck passed by on the dirt road along the fence. The sprinklers kept time with the spirit of the water while a bee weaved in and out of the window beside my left ear. It was hot.

The sick, stirring feeling in my gut made me wonder if my face looked like Bruce's that day I left him at the airport. How do you describe that look? When two young lovers separate, even one day feels like an eternity. Your face cringes and you feel helpless, and empty inside.

We walked this road together the day after we were married, June 14, 1968. The sun was shining on a beautiful, warm, clear day.

"This is where I want to be buried," I remembered him saying, though I could not remember the sound of his voice. We had been walking arm in arm with the moun-

We Regret to Inform You

tains in our view. The words caught me off guard; after all, we had just gotten married! We had visited the grave of Bruce's Uncle Bruce who served in World War I.

Now, every time I visit the cemetery I walk the same path.

Bruce, I'm going to face a dragon today. I'm going to see a film called 'Regret to Inform.'

Those were the words they said when they told me you were dead. They didn't say the word "dead," though. They said you were "critically wounded." I think that's what they said, or maybe it was "fatally wounded"—I don't remember.

This time, I want you to come with me when I go for my walk. You know I walk this path every time I come here. Come with me this time, Bruce. Let's walk it together. Maybe you can *help me remember what it felt like to be 19.*

Tears seeped from my eyes.

Why didn't I say anything when you told me you wanted to be buried here? Why didn't I tell you not to go? Why didn't I cry then? Why did I try to act so brave? It was so long ago, Bruce. Now I am old and you are still young. It's like you stopped in time.

I felt sick, it was hot and I was sobbing.

Remember the funeral home director? He tried to talk me out of buying my burial plot next to yours. He said something like "The 'normal' thing that usually happens is that people move on with their lives, get remarried." I refused to hear it. I knew that's what you wanted for me, too. Remember, in California you made me promise that if anything ever happened to you I would get remarried? When you were persistent, I said I would.

I lied.

The thought was too foreign, I couldn't imagine myself getting remarried. I just didn't want you to worry about it. I knew my own mind...then. Your memory still lives Bruce, even though I tried so hard to bury it with you.

A breeze picked up and tossed my hair, bringing a smile through the tears.

You taught me to enjoy letting the wind blow through my hair. I came from a heavy-duty hair spray world until you came along.

Tired and hot, I knew it was time to wipe the tears and move on. The somber, daydream-state-of-mind stayed with me as I checked into the small, cabin-like motel room.

What am I supposed to find here: myself?

We Regret to Inform You

Wow, the dagger will be drawn from my heart today, then what?

When my wound is healed, then what do I do? I know my world is going to change dramatically, but how?

I took a short nap before going to the grocery store. It was still hot outside and not real cool inside. I guessed that's the difference in the price of a room.

How do I feel?

I wasn't sure, only that I felt like I wasn't really there.

I drove around town and looked at the familiar sights, including a church I had attended on one of my previous visits. My soul was asking for help, but no one seemed to see the need. By putting a smile on my face I could fool them every time.

I pulled beside what I thought was a park and realized it was the courthouse when I saw a police officer enter the building. (Bruce had wanted to be a State Police officer like the father he never knew.)

I couldn't imagine who in this town would show up for this film. Mothers, I suppose, people like me who had lost someone. *How many of us could there possibly be?*

I drove to the head of Wallowa Lake and felt calm as long as I concentrated on my natural surroundings. I passed an empty pasture and a pasture with horses, and in the town of Joseph I saw a bronze statue of a horse. I wondered if people think that a statue of a horse is more beautiful than a real horse in on open field.

I felt sick again.

What am I doing coming all this way to see a film?

I remembered the film title, "Regret to Inform." When

those words were spoken to me three decades ago, I became, in effect, a prisoner of war. The Vietnam war came to my door; I was wounded, taken prisoner and beaten down for 33 years.

Now I was here to face my captor. I would not be defeated this time! Fear and confidence struggled for control of my thoughts. By managing to stay calm all day, I figured I had been handling things well. This would be a piece of cake, I thought.

If you have ever had a surgery, you know there comes the time when you let go and turn your life over to the surgeon and the operating staff. Time for the film was closing in and I was getting nervous. I felt like I was preparing for an athletic event.

All day my thoughts had been just thoughts. Now, it was time to put on the armor and go into action. I put my clothes on the bed and showered, thinking it would help. Instead, my senses began to scramble. By the time I was dressed I was in a panic.

The ugly demons of fear and insecurity reared their heads in a last attempt to keep me in the familiar zone of emotional captivity.

My God, "Regret to Inform." *I have to go there and face those horrific, painful words.*

Facing them would help to heal my heart, but then

We Regret to Inform You

what? *I'm used to living with the dagger buried in scar tissue. Maybe I can just accept the wellness I have attained so far and just not do this. I don't know how seeing this film will change me. At least I am familiar with living with the pain. What will life be like when the pain is gone?*

God, I can't do this. I can't, I just can't.

My mind raged back and forth.

Don't go.

Yes, go slay the dragon once and for all.

I felt like I was preparing to go up against a giant.

I paced back and forth like a caged animal in the small, stale motel room.

There was something familiar about this experience: I was wrestling the feelings of hopelessness, helplessness and defeat as they clawed their way to the surface. Without realizing it, I was feeling the same emotions that I faced the morning of September 14, 1968, just before they told me Bruce was dead. I couldn't stop the process then, and I couldn't stop it now. I could not stop those two Marines from telling me Bruce was dead, just like I could not stop Bruce from dying. I knew that if I wanted to heal I had to feel the pain.

I can't do it.

The feeling of helplessness reared its head. My face was wet with tears, sweat or both.

How, can I do this?

I unthinkingly leaned over, clutching my stomach, just as I did over 30 years ago.

GOD, *you said you wouldn't give me more than I can handle–I...CAN'T...DO...THIS! This is more than I can handle.*

Sacred Shadow, Sacred Ground

It was almost time to go.

What will I find there? What will I have to say? I'll have to be around other people.

Tears dammed for so many years want to burst forth. *What if I cry in public? I'm already crying.*

GOD, *it's too much.* I CAN'T DO THIS ALONE!

I sat in the chair beside the door and took a deep breath. I was beginning to talk myself out of going when the words entered my mind: **"You don't have to go alone, you don't have to do anything but show up."**

Those thoughts quieted my spirit and I began to breathe easier as I remembered God would not desert me. This event was orchestrated by a power higher than myself.

God is the surgeon I would trust to extract the dagger buried in my heart.

Okay, God, if that is all I have to do, I can do that. I'll show up. I won't talk to anyone. I'll sit quietly, watch the film and come back to my room.

I can do that, and that's ALL I CAN DO.

As I drove to the theater, my fear began to dissipate and determination to see this through grew stronger. The showing of the film would be accompanied by a talk by one of the widows featured in the film. Xuan Ngoc Nguyen, a widow of a South Vietnamese soldier, would speak after the film.

The man standing just inside the door of the old historic theater was the one who had arranged to have the film shown in Enterprise. I pretended to be cool, calm and collected as I greeted him and worked my way through the lobby.

It was early enough that I could easily choose an aisle seat close to the doorway. It was more than a convenience; it was a need to be close to an escape route.

I watched as people began to enter, hoping to see a familiar face. I didn't know anyone.

I was on my own, but not alone, God was with me.

A small-framed woman with long black hair entered the room, surrounded by people.

The way she walked and smiled so easily reminded me of my therapist. *Man, I wish my therapist would show up.*

I watched as she and her companion sat two rows in front of me. *This is the woman who is going to speak.* I couldn't help but think, *My God, she is beautiful.*

I don't remember if she talked before the film or after it or both. I watched with the focus of an alcoholic's narrowed vision and breathed in every word.

Young people going up and down the aisle irritated me. This was my life they are talking about here, I wanted to hear every word. I wanted everyone to sit down, be still and listen.

Xuan's story was filled with more horrific experiences than I could imagine. She was a widow who lived "in-country" during the war the Vietnamese call the *American War.*

Connecting with part of her story made me feel like I was being introduced to myself.

I too, am a widow of the Vietnam War.

Isn't that what they told me 33 years ago when they brought the war to my doorstep and said the words "Regret to Inform"?

Am I just now getting it?

My throat tightened as I choked back tears that tried to seep through. I struggled to hide the agony I felt as the transformation began to take place within me.

I am a war widow.

During the month Bruce was in Vietnam, he must have killed people. It was hard for me to imagine that he could kill another human being. He was a rifleman on the front line, that was his job. A part of me was thankful he did not have to spend an entire year experiencing the atrocities of war.

I made it through the showing without making a spectacle of myself. I maintained my composure. After the film was over, Xuan, a petite woman with a heavy-duty story, told more about her personal experience and took questions from the audience. I looked around, wondering if there were other Vietnam war widows in the audience, since I didn't see any women who looked as stricken as I felt.

There were veterans whose questions seemed to turn the conversation around to a Vietnam veteran's point of view.

I wanted to say, "Wait a minute, we have our own story to tell as widows of the Vietnamese-American War. We were hurt, too."

We Regret to Inform You

I felt disturbed at this, without consciously making a decision to do so, I was taking ownership of my identity.

The audience treated Xuan with great respect, and when she finished she came back down the steps into the aisle. It was over! I could leave! I did what God wanted me to do, I showed up. As I stood up to leave I realized the dagger in my heart wasn't really gone at all. I saw Xuan a few steps away from me and I thought I should thank her for sharing her story.

Instead, I started for the doorway.

What if you're the only other Vietnam War widow in the audience? It took a lot of courage to do what she did. **Go! Thank her!**

She turned as I tapped her on the shoulder.

"Thank you for sharing your story."

As soon as I said those words, by the look on her face, I knew I had to say more. The words were awkward and strange to my voice.

I released the words, "I'm a widow of Vietnam, too."

She reached to give me a hug. I heard her say, "No more war," as we embraced, and I responded, "No more war."

Suddenly it was more than a hug between two people. It was an embrace between two countries.

It wasn't until later in my motel room that I realized the importance of that brief interaction. Speaking the words, "I am a widow of Vietnam, too," opened the wound; the embrace between two countries cauterized it.

The transition going on inside me made me not want to talk to anyone, but at the same time I wanted to talk to everyone.

I had been shaken by facing the dragon.

As I made my way to the lobby, I realized I didn't want to be alone just yet. I mingled and talked to Rich, the organizer. I wanted to buy a sweatshirt that said, "The Legacy of Vietnam" but had to wait until the next day. Rich invited me to stop by the local bookstore on my way out of town.

For the first time I openly introduced myself as a Vietnam War widow without feeling I would bleed to death from the wound in my heart. The stigma of Vietnam had also lifted. It was a strange thing to be able to say who I was and not fear rejection.

I went back to my motel room still digesting the information and experience of that night. God took care of the situation. The dragon had been slain, the dagger removed.

I was able to sleep peacefully and the next day, while waiting for Rich at the book store, I come across another book, *Grief Denied: A Vietnam Widow's Story*, by Pauline Laurent. To date, it was the only book I had found that had been written by another Vietnam War widow. The title alone grasped me by the neck and said, "Read me."

It not only summed up what I had been doing for over 30 years, denying my grief, but it spoke to my identity. I, too, am a widow of the Vietnam War.

We Regret to Inform You

On the way out of town I stopped by the cemetery to place flowers on Bruce's headstone. I felt rushed when I saw there were people close by. They were there for a funeral.

I had not had time to digest all the feelings that come with the previous day's experience. I was hoping to do some of it at the cemetery. Instead, I felt I should move on and let those of another family have the privacy to mourn their loss.

Bruce, I'm going to leave you these flowers. I am so sorry that I neglected your memory. I love you, and I love your memory.

I am a different person today. The world is the same, but how I view the world has changed overnight.

Pain is universal. Like Xuan said, "Salty tears taste the same no matter what country you are from."

The sun's warmth caressed me as I knelt to place the flowers on the headstone that says, "For those who fight for it, life has a taste the protected will never know."

I acknowledged to myself and to Bruce,

This trip was not just about you dying. These flowers are for both of us, 'cause I lost me when I lost you.

I left the cemetery in quiet resignation. I knew there were more tears to cry, but I felt God's strength walking inside me. I felt a sense of victory, and accomplishment, in having won a major conflict in my personal war.

Sacred Shadow, Sacred Ground

Like collecting scattered wildflowers among tall grasses on a mountain hillside, I gather memories to put into my memorial bouquet that will pay homage to the losses of my past.

—Glenda M. Carter

Sacred Shadow, Sacred Ground

I could tell that my dad was especially proud that night. I saw him on the front steps of the church after the wedding. He had a big smile and a certain way of flicking the ashes from his cigarette that said, "Job well done."

And the day came when the risk it took to remain tight inside the bud was more painful than the risk it took to blossom.

— Anais Nin

Through The Valley of Grief and Losses

Sacred Shadow, Sacred Ground

In 1968, when Bruce and I decided to get married before he left for Vietnam, we did so knowing there wasn't much time to plan a wedding. However, friends and family gathered around and helped to put together a small ceremony held in our community Assembly Of God Church.

People who came were church, work and family friends, my parents, brothers, their wives and other extended family members. Bruce's mother had died only three months earlier and in an attempt to keep things simple he did not include a long list of guests.

My longtime friend Diane came to my rescue by lending me the wedding dress that she wore just months before. Her father, the pastor of our church, performed the ceremony while she stood by my side as matron of honor. Diane was like a big sister.

Her husband, Hank, was in the Army and already in Vietnam. He and Bruce never met. At 18 and 19 years old, we all were still inexperienced kids trying to make adult decisions that included Vietnam.

Diane and I shared common ground. We married in the same year, and both of our husbands went to Vietnam. One came home in a casket, the other in body; however, we both lost the men we sent away.

Two months after we were married Bruce was in Vietnam. One month later he was killed in battle.

Through the Valley of Grief and Losses

Our lives unfolded rapidly and were just as quickly hidden away in the deep caverns of my mind. My recollections of that period are foggy.

For a while, friends and family remained in my life, but they did so with the quiet understanding that we just did not talk about Bruce. Stuffing memories included turning my back on life-long friends whose presence triggered emotions I fought to bury.

During a recent phone conversation, I told Diane that I was having problems remembering that time of my life. She was able to fill in some of the blanks. After Bruce's body had arrived home, every night until after the funeral I called and asked her to go with me to the mortuary. We sat beside Bruce's casket and talked until closing time.

Until she reminded me, I had been thinking, *I wish I would have sat with him.*

Now, I know I did.

She also reminded me that I feared that it might not really be Bruce in the casket.

Bruce had told me before he left that if he was severely wounded, he would not come home but would remain living abroad. Not only did I experience the normal denial, but I felt an urgency to know if it really was him in the closed, flag-draped casket. For all I knew, he could have been burned beyond recognition and the dog tags could have been switched or lost. My mind searched for a scenario that could justify my fear.

At first we were told that we could not view Bruce's body, that his casket should remain closed.

My father, who lost his brother in World War II,

stopped by the funeral home on his way home from work and convinced the funeral director to allow him to view Bruce.

He needed the peace of knowing for sure.

When I found out they let my father view him I went directly to the funeral home intent on seeing Bruce. It angered me that anyone would try to make the decision for me as to whether I should see him or not. No one could protect me from dealing with the reality that my husband lay in that casket. Seeing him could not be worse than the fact he was dead.

Out of love for me, my father and mother tried to protect me and to get me to change my mind, but it made me more determined. They could not deter my need to see the person I was suppose to spend the rest of my life with.

I believe that my fierce sense of responsibility for Bruce was what kept me from killing myself.

I had never seen him in his Marine "dress blues" before. His head and hands were wrapped in white; they resembled the wrapping of a mummy. He was tall and very thin. I looked for something familiar, some way of identifying him.

The mortician pulled the sleeve of his left arm above his wrist and looked at me as if I could confirm it was Bruce by seeing a three inch patch of skin. I nodded. It was the color of his skin. It was more confirmation than I had previously.

Struggling to maintain composure, I thanked the mortician, turned and walked away.

It must have hurt my parents to see me walk numbly by

Through the Valley of Grief and Losses

them as I left the building. They could not console nor comfort me—no one could.

Interment was at the Enterprise Cemetery about 80 miles from home. I could not imagine following the hearse, so I asked if I could ride with the driver. My oldest brother Claude gritted his teeth and accompanied me on the journey. He and the driver made small talk and tried to include me in the conversation as we drove the same road Bruce and I had driven the night of our wedding. What did it matter to me that the sun was shinning or that the trees were turning fall colors? It was futile.

I could tell being in a hearse with a dead body was wearing on my brother's nerves; for me it was my place to be. Perhaps it was the part of me that wanted to go to the grave with him. My focus had not changed; I concentrated on getting through the graveside portion of the funeral service. I hadn't thought of what would come later.

A small group gathered around the casket at the cemetery. My body was there but my mind was searching for the best way to escape.

It must be over, the Marines are folding the flag. They worked with precision and made it look like the one they gave to Jackie Kennedy.

What did they say? My eyes widened as the young Marine walked toward me. He handed me the folded flag. I clutched it to my chest tightly, as if I were applying pressure to keep the blood from spurting from the open wound in my heart. It's over. It was quiet. Now what? I don't know what to do now. I wanted to run away. I wasn't able to speak and it felt like people were staring at me. I didn't want to see the sympathetic look in their eyes. I turned quickly to walk away.

Bruce's cousin asked me if I was okay. "Yes," I lied. My brother, still gritting his teeth, came with me. We walked a short distance on that familiar path Bruce and I had walked. People respected my space and did not try to offer condolences I could not accept.

Now what do I do?

I was unable to allow anyone to comfort me, I felt lost and alone.

When I think back, I wish I would have cried and hugged everyone there. I wish I could have acknowledged and shared the loss we all felt.

As we drove down the hill I looked back and saw Bruce's casket, alone, perched above ground. He looked as alone as I felt. "Until death do you part..." echoed through the empty chambers of my heart. I was suppose to let go now. But I still loved him—how could I magically let go? Death took his body, but not my love. A part of me was about to be buried with him and I did not know how to stop that from happening.

For the first time I allowed my family to see me cry.

My other brother Doug and his wife were in the back seat and I saw the pain in his eyes as he shut off his own tears. They all looked so uncomfortable that I forced myself to stop crying.

Through the Valley of Grief and Losses

We drove to Wallow Lake. I expected it would be the same as it was in June when Bruce and I were there. Instead, a small boy walking with his dog greeted us as we drove into the park area. It was the end of tourist season. It was empty, like me.

They had not finished lowering Bruce into his grave by the time we returned to the cemetery. Doug, my brother who tries so hard to smooth things out, nervously talked as if trying to convince me we should leave and let them finish their work. I knew he was trying to protect me from seeing them put Bruce into the ground.

How we got home and what happened for the next few months is lost in my memory.

With Hank still in Vietnam, Diane and I spent a lot of evenings just driving around talking about whatever, with no particular place to go. Gasoline prices in 1969 were only about .35 a gallon, so it was nothing to drive to the next town and back. It helped me keep my mind off the pain, and helped keep her mind off worrying about Hank.

My withdrawal began when they told me Bruce was killed and continued to deepen as I stuffed my feelings down and locked them away in my self-made prison. If I talked about Vietnam at all, it would have been with Diane; however, I don't recall any discussions about the war.

Sacred Shadow, Sacred Ground

By the time Hank returned home in 1969, I was not able to wholeheartedly celebrate his homecoming. I felt angry when I visited them. Anger was a part of a grief process that I knew nothing about. I didn't understand the displaced feelings of resentment and why I felt cheated. How could I possibly be mad at Hank for coming home from Vietnam and at the same time feel thankful? The feelings didn't make sense and because I kept them to myself, no one could explain them to me.

With Hank home, Diane and I spent less time together. One of the last times I visited with them was when they brought their first child by my parents' home, where I was still living. It was too painful. They reminded me of the life I didn't have. They reminded me that Bruce was dead.

From outward appearances it seemed that they were getting on with their lives. In the struggle to ease my pain, I abandoned our friendship. I had no understanding that the course of their lives had been as disrupted as my own.

We were strangers for the next 30 years.

The unpopularity of the Vietnam War made it easy for me to avoid the subject. No one really wanted to talk about it.

In the fall of 1969, I enrolled in a two-year college—the first of my several attempts to get a college education—and tried to figure out what to do with my life.

One of the subjects I took was a course in sociology, and Vietnam was a hot topic on campus at that time. I don't remember anything about the class except the final

Through the Valley of Grief and Losses

exam. When I read the question about Vietnam, I could not respond. I wrote a note on the test and told the instructor that I could not deal with the subject of the Vietnam War. I told him my husband had been killed there and I could not complete the test. When I turned it in, I felt defeated, ashamed and like an incompetent failure. He passed me with a 'D'.

One of Bruce's high school classmates was also a student. Blanche and I became friends and sometimes hang out together. I don't remember if we ever discussed Bruce.

I developed a happy-go-lucky persona which fooled most people. I left school after the incident in the sociology class and returned to work at the nursing home in Milton-Freewater.

It wasn't until the writing of this book that Blanche and I reconnected. I was able to ask her what Bruce was like when he was in high school. She affirmed that he was as good as I thought he was when I met him. He was honorable, smart, and a real true friend. In our last phone conversation we both agreed that if there were more people like him our world would not be in such a mess. Blanche finished her education, married, had children and a career working for the county. She now has two beautiful grandchildren she adores.

As for myself, I continued to roam from place to place, functioning in survival mode.

Most days, I had to find a reason to live. After two other attempts to return to college I finally earned my first Associate of Science Degree in Applied Photography

Sacred Shadow, Sacred Ground

in 1978.

College provided me with flexibility, stability and a positive atmosphere in which to survive. As a student, one can act a little strange and be considered normal.

Photography was the creative process that allowed me a needed versatility.

The year after graduation I fell into a deeper depression. All the positive influences from college had lost their effect. I was suicidal. After recovering from gall bladder surgery in 1979 or early 1980, I challenged God. The emotional pain was just too great. My soul was tormented. While holding an air-filled syringe to the vein in my arm I cried and demanded, GOD! TELL ME ONE GOOD REASON WHY I SHOULD NOT KILL MYSELF!

The answer I got surprised me.

"Because by the time that air bubble reaches your heart, I'll have shown you what you will have missed and you'll be sorry, but it will be too late for you to change your mind."

I still had enough faith in God to believe that God could and would actually do that.

It was a decisive moment. I threw the syringe away. My struggle with depression and suicide continued but was not as severe. The syringe episode encouraged me to live.

When I moved to California a few months later, I started another life. Being away from my home town allowed me the freedom to ask for help. Connecting with people and escaping my identity of a war widow helped me to function. The suicidal veil lifted along with the depression. Life was manageable. No one knew about my life with

Through the Valley of Grief and Losses

Bruce. I could hide in the city and become whomever I wanted to be without the scrutiny of people who knew me. But after three years, the longing to be where I could see the mountains and sky became overpowering. Thus, I returned to eastern Oregon.

My life had improved, I was no longer suicidal. I found jobs that did not require long-term commitment. However, it wasn't long until the familiarity of my home town triggered my depression. The life improvements I thought I had made began to wither away because they were based on my false self.

When I felt my depression worsening and suicidal thoughts returning, I went back to the most familiar, positive atmosphere I knew: I returned to college. It was still unthinkable for me to get counseling and admit that I was "crazy." Instead, I decided to major in psychology and took a class about grief and loss.

It was 1987, and for the first time I understood there was something called a grief process. I learned to apply the new knowledge to my life, addressing my current problems instead of stuffing them on top of the old ones.

It was also the year my father died. I shared my new knowledge with my mother and we were able to grieve the loss of my father more openly and timely.

Life remained difficult, but college life served as my therapy and provided me with a sense of belonging and a place to excel. Although photography opened up creative opportunities for me, I can honestly say that my major course of study in college was "Survival." Had I had a plan, I would have earned at least one master's degree from all the credits I accumulated.

By 1991, I had finally earned a Bachelor of Science degree (B.S.) in General Studies.

While working toward that degree I saw Margaret, a school nurse practitioner, regarding my weight problem. I felt as if I was lost on a raft, drifting around on a cesspool. I had lost faith in humanity. I pretended I was alive.

Margaret became the bright light that guided me ashore. She was kind, gentle and compassionate. She treated me with acceptance and respect.

She never preached a word, but her silent witness brought me hope and let me know that God had not forsaken me. Cautiously, I began to let her see some of the emotional pain I was carrying. When I told her about Bruce, she cried.

For a year and a half, Margaret was my lifeline. She helped restore my faith in God and humanity. Our time together was dependent on my being a student. When the time came to an end, she taught me how to say good-bye. I gave her a copy of a book by Richard Bach, *There's No Such Place As Far Away*.

You would have a hard time convincing me that she was anything less than an angel.

After graduation I started seeing a therapist and continued to do so until I moved from the area in 1992.

For a few years I worked as a drug and alcohol abuse counselor. My work gave me a sense of identity I had not known before. However, after five years, I began to suffer the effects of job "burnout."

Through the Valley of Grief and Losses

Once again I became a non-productive, irresponsible, lazy human being in the eyes of society. Once again I lost my sense of identity. The social perks that came with working for a county agency were gone. Taking a less prestigious job signaled failure to new friends.

I felt ashamed and humiliated as I slipped back into my survival mode. To survive, I sought a job that would not require a long-term commitment or mental challenges. A minimum wage job was not sufficient to maintain the lifestyle to which I had become accustomed, so I began to deplete my savings. I was on my last descent.

I did not realize at that time that I suffered from a condition called Post Traumatic Stress Disorder (PTSD). Even after working with clients who obviously had PTSD, I could not see myself with this disabling condition. I had surrounded myself with people whose lives were chaotic. I was able to ignore my problems by concentrating on theirs. I minimized, justified, and denied myself until I hit bottom.

There was no where to go, no one to blame and I could not pretend any longer. I was beaten.

When I returned to my therapist in 2001 for help with my chronic depression, she made the diagnosis: I was suffering from PTSD. In prior sessions, I had avoided the subject of Bruce. I was still in denial over the impact it had on my life. Until the diagnosis, I could not figure out the focus point. Something was wrong, but what was it? If you don't know which illness you have, how do you treat it?

I read as much data about PTSD as I could find. As I began to understand it, I become determined to stop it from controlling my life. For the first time I understood why I was so emotionally disconnected. I understood that I was not the only person who has the problem of PTSD. I did not want to admit or accept it, but by honestly looking at this condition, my past behaviors begin to make sense. I found the will to fight back. If you are told you have cancer, you get treatment if you want to live. It is the same with PTSD. After acceptance I was able to say, Okay, I have it; now, how do I fix it?

I was angry. I was tired of living with the shame and guilt that comes with not being able to truly function in society because of this debilitating condition.

After talking with veterans and wives of veterans who returned from Vietnam, I began to think about Diane and Hank. I wondered how the war had affected them and if they knew about PTSD. I wanted to share the information and progress of my recovery.

Several years ago, Diane was working in a department store about a hundred miles away. I decided to make that my first stop in finding her. Nervously, I asked a store clerk if Diane still worked there.

She did. While waiting for her to come from her office, I pictured her as she was when we were in our 20's. I could see her smile and hear her laugh.

Memory fools us, allowing us to see things as they were when last visited. Mine was playing its trick; I was looking for the same Diane I knew 30 years ago.

It was a strange feeling to meet the past while in the present, or was I meeting the present while in the past? How many life-times, how many conversations can be had or missed in a 30-year period? Where did all the time go? Adjusting to my new reality was like coming out of a dark cave into the light after many years of seclusion. My memory was being set free, free from my self-imposed prison.

Several years earlier I had written a story for a creative writing class, set inside a prison.

The teacher asked if she could read it aloud. As she read I could see her shiver as if the words were running up and down her spine.

An older woman in our class leaned over to me when the reading was finished and asked, "How do you know so much about prison?"

The answer I gave her was not the truth, because I didn't really know the truth. However, I asked myself later, "How do I know so much about prison?" It was one time my subconscious had attempted an escape by using symbolism.

During my meeting with Diane, I wasn't sure how to approach the truths. For the first time in many years I wanted to talk about real life issues and reconnect with my friends. But would my friends want to reconnect with me? Would Diane forgive me for abandoning her? I knew in my heart it was time to let go of the protective false self I had created and dare to be real. When it was my turn to answer the "How are you?" question, I began to tell her the truth.

I told her that after all these years I had been diagnosed with PTSD; and during the previous year, I worked through a lot of my unresolved grief and loss issues along with the condition of Post Traumatic Stress Disorder. I told her that life was beginning to make sense after a name had been put to the patterns of my behavior. I told her how I had tried to bury the memories of Bruce and Vietnam. She listened and responded with a sense of familiarity that led me to believe she really understood.

Diane had not mentioned Hank, but I was not prepared for the answer she gave when I asked about him. It was like running into a brick wall when she said they divorced a couple of years ago.

I knew from a conversation I had with another wife of a returned Vietnam veteran that life was not the same when her husband came home from battle. Elenor was the wife of "Ski," the squad leader that led Bruce and the others the night of the ambush.

When she and I spoke, she told me of his horrible death. He lost his battle with alcohol and other drug addictions and suffered the last years of his life curling back into the fetal position until he died. She also shared with me some of the horrific abuses she had survived.

Elenor very gently told me, "You are the lucky one, you

just don't know it." In that moment I stopped thinking and just listened. The tone in her voice and the care she took while speaking the words made me listen. It was more than a passing comment; it was a message that I would not fully comprehend until later.

I had only shared the beginning part of Diane's and Hank's lives together. Just like Bruce and I, they were young and in love, with hopes and dreams for the future. Hank did not come home the same innocent young man she married.

"It was like living with someone I didn't know. The Hank I married died over there, I just didn't have the body to bury in the ground."

He had not shown a lot of interest in talking about Vietnam except when he had been drinking. She went on to say that his behavior affected their sons. Their father was not emotionally available.

She told me that Hank had been in an engineering unit and often was called out to do other duties, like carry bodies off the battlefield.

I asked her to tell him for me to go to a counselor or a doctor and see if he is suffering from PTSD. She told me that he had gone to counseling at one time where PTSD was discussed.

Within our brief conversation I was not able to comprehend that he had already had a diagnosis of PTSD. For me the diagnosis itself was a main factor in my ability to get better, but it is not always that way for other people.

She assured me she would talk to Hank and within minutes I was returning home. I told her I would mail her information on PTSD and anything else I could find that would help her and her family.

How did we get so old? We are in our 50's—how did we get here? I wondered. I knew life had taken its toll. Diane didn't smile as easily as she used to; in fact, she hardly smiled at all. She seemed somber even before we began to talk about the serious events of our life.

I'm not sure if it was the words of understanding or how she spoke them that led me to believe that underneath her serious demeanor remained a positive outlook on life. It was the same sense of strength she shared with me so many years ago. It did not dawn on me that her understanding was from personal experience.

My emotions were mixed as I drove away. My past and present were in conflict until I submitted to reality. I was wrong, they had not escaped the aftermath of the war.

It was after this visit that I truly began to grieve the loss of friendships. I knew we had abandoned each other; our emotional wounds had caused us to live in a mode of survival in a world where it was not okay to talk about our problems. I was deeply saddened to hear of their divorce, since it represented yet another casualty of Vietnam.

Without further contact, I began to write my book, about a year later. I had not planned to write about old friends. Their divorce weighed heavily on my heart. The four of us all lost our lives. They hadn't just magically picked up and gone on with their life. It wasn't a fairy tale where they lived "happily ever after."

Through the process of re-connecting with friends, I have learned a serious lesson. The loss of Bruce in battle was not

Through the Valley of Grief and Losses

any harder or any easier than having a husband return home emotionally wounded and lost. Loss is loss and hardship is hardship and we each have our cross to bear.

Elenor's words began to ring true.

Through a phone conversation with Hank, he affirmed that he was previously diagnosed with PTSD, but was not currently seeking treatment for that condition. He was diagnosed with Diabetes II from exposure to Agent Orange and has had a pacemaker put in to regulate his heart. He talked about going to the Vietnam War Memorial in Washington, D. C., and mentioned he would like to go back to Vietnam. He is a veteran who continues to struggle to find his way home.

Hank was not physically wounded in Vietnam, but his heart, mind and soul were rearranged like the mangled soldiers he carried off the battlefield.

"Hank was not the same person," Diane said, "he died over there. He came back in a body we called Hank, but he wasn't in it. It was like living with the walking dead."

How do families recover from living with the walking dead? In the process of life they are damaged as well. Where are the support systems for them? Diane suffers from her own physical problems and financial challenges. At almost 60 years old she is forced to re-enter the work force. Where are the health benefits for the widows of the walking dead?

Our phone conversations have become more relaxed in sharing the loss of ourselves.

We are becoming reacquainted. We laugh together like old times, and strangely enough, the sound of her voice and positive way of looking at things often remind me of how her friendship brought me strength.

Diane has helped me to travel through the valley of grief for the loss of friendships as I make my way home.

If not for the Vietnam war, would the four of us have been lifelong friends who shared growth and maturity of living? I guess it is another question for the wind.

I don't waste time on the what ifs; it is as it is.

"I can still picture us...young again."

"Ambushed" Disclaimer

I do not pretend to know how a Vietnam veteran may feel, but thanks to the openness and willingness of the Marines who shared their stories with me, I have a better understanding of how Bruce lived and died in Vietnam. After 35 years I can stop wondering.

The following three sections were compiled from information I gathered from letters, reports, and personal phone interviews of Marines who were at or near Liberty Bridge, *Quang Nam* Province, Vietnam the night Bruce was killed.

Please take into consideration that Marines in Bruce's battalion, some from different companies, were positioned at various viewpoints within the scope of a greater battlefield, and their memories have been affected by time and events.

I have done my best to verify each event, and to respectfully and accurately interpret the information I have been provided.

Boys to Men

Young boys hiding in a field,
stick weapons pointed like guns.
Surprise! Bang! Bang! you're dead.

Fall down. You are dead.
Laugh, Chuckle, We won!
Get up, do it all over again.

My hat is white, yours is black,
I'm the good guy, you're the bad.
Surprise! Bang! Bang! you're dead.

Fall down. You are dead.
Laugh, Chuckle,
We won.

Young men hiding in a field.
Live ammo, real guns.
Surprise, Bang! Bang! you're dead.

They fell down
They did not get up
We won! Do it all over again.

Hide and seek.
Sneak and hide.
Surprise! Bang! Bang! you're dead.

We fell down.
We did not get up.
My brothers cried.

Ambushed

Sacred Shadow, Sacred Ground

> *"I didn't get put with a Recon unit, so don't worry about me getting hurt."*
>
> — Letter from Bruce, August 16, 1968

After arriving in Vietnam on the 13th of August, Bruce was one of many replacements sent to Foxtrot Company, 2nd Battalion, 5th Marines, 1st Marine Division, a highly-decorated battalion of an elite group of men.

On August 19, 1968, he arrived near Liberty Bridge at *Phu Loc 6* where Fox Company shared the high ground with a USMC 105mm howitzer battery. Fox Company had three primary missions: to protect both sides of the bridge; to prevent the enemy from setting mines on a two and one-half mile stretch of road from Liberty Bridge to *An Hoa*; and to provide mutual support for the battery.

Liberty Bridge had already been destroyed, but this was the site where supply truck convoys crossed the river by barge.

Watching the nightly news became the ritual in our house. Intently glued to the TV screen, my father and I watched in hopes of seeing a glimpse of Bruce.

> *"I'm setting here on top of this hill where our camp is, it over looks the prettiest and one of the biggest valleys you have ever seen. You would really fall in love with this place it is so pretty."*
>
> — August 25, 1968

Every day men were being wounded and killed. The television reports made it sound as though there weren't

Ambushed

many casualties, but August 1968 was a period of increased losses.

There is still controversy about whether the actual number of WIA (wounded-in-action) and KIA (killed-in-action) were truthfully reported to the American people.

Many of my sources say the numbers were skewed and that casualty report numbers were falsified at the time, for political reasons.

Some Marines had pictures they had taken confiscated before they returned home and many letters were censored. They were given specific orders not to tell their positions, share what military operation they were involved in, or tell how many of their comrades were killed or wounded. However, a couple of times Bruce mentioned battlefield losses.

> *"We lost six men today, 1 dead, five pretty well done in. One was our squad M-79 man the others were 1st squad. We were all good friends. It isn't good to think about it, but then there it is, so what is one to do?"*
>
> — August 27, 1968
>
> *"We lost another four men yesterday. In five days we've lost over 30 % of our platoon..."*
>
> — September 1, 1968

Being wounded three times could have meant a ticket back to the United States; however, this rule was often ignored and men were sent back into battle if they were capable of fighting.

Bruce tried to maintain a positive outlook, but I could tell there was a lot about his reality that he was not sharing with me. We were both beginning to recognize the seriousness of the situation we were in.

We assured each other over and over of the sincerity of our love in our letters. It was as though every "I Love You" could be our last. He swore that when he came home he would never leave me again. The word forever was still in our vocabulary.

How else do you subconsciously prepare to lose or leave someone you love, for eternity?

> *"After being separated for so long every moment we have together will be one to be treasured and not to be taken for granted..."*
> — September 3, 1968

Because he could not share his day-to-day activities openly, his letters focused on the love we shared, memories we built together and the dreams for our future. He talked often about how grateful he was for our relationship and our shared faith in God. It was these thoughts and his belief in God that sustained him.

> *"I was reading the part in the Bible about heaven last night and it makes all this hellish way of life seem bearable."*
> — September 3, 1968.

People around him were killing and being killed. I did not want to think of Bruce getting killed, nor did I want

Ambushed

to think about him killing another human being. In order to survive, a warrior must justify and maintain a "kill or be killed" mindset. I couldn't help wondering what long-term effect this would have on him.

They were just boys hiding in fields, waiting to surprise the other group of boys. Like playing cops and robbers, cowboys and Indians, when they were small children.

Suddenly the rules had changed. A boy's dream came true. Imaginary weapons became lethal fire power. They could shoot real guns, drive real tanks, fire real rockets. Patriotic flames burned in their soul while pride ran through their veins.

Friends united together to carry out the duty of killing the enemy.

They could come home American heroes like their fathers and grandfathers had done from World War I and World War II. After all, we were the good, they were the bad.

Instead, our country was in major transition. We were coming out of the '50s, the age of innocence.

On the home front, the early '60s brought the assassination of our President. It was a time we thought the President of the United States was invincible. He was a great man, someone to aspire to. John F. Kennedy was shot and killed while riding in an open car motorcade in Dallas, Texas. It left the nation in shock and stricken with grief.

After 40 years there are still many of us who lived through that ordeal who do not believe the assassination was carried out by one person. I encourage you to review the history of the 60's. It is a fascinating study.

Moving on with my own story, the war in Vietnam produced more loss of life. More grief. Leaders with peaceful ideals were gunned down and killed before our eyes. I don't remember seeing anyone killed on television until the Kennedy assassination and Lee Harvey Oswald was shot down by Jack Ruby in retaliation.

For the first time in history, television was used to play the scene of murder over and over, searing it into our minds. The visual reinforcement was the beginning of the desensitization of our nation. The trauma was relived in the minds of older adults and children.

The media helped to shape our world in the 60's by repeatedly reporting in vivid detail the disasters and murders that were changing our world.

In those days, Post Traumatic Stress Disorder, (PTSD) had not been identified. It was years later that the name was finally attached to the condition; in previous wars it was simply called "shell shock."

People with PTSD often relive the scene of trauma, as it uncontrollably plays over and over in their minds. It is a lot like being overly saturated with news reports on television, only worse.

In 1968, the civil rights leader, Martin Luther King Jr., and Senator Robert Kennedy, a presidential candidate and brother of President Kennedy, were assassinated on camera.

It was the same year Bruce was killed, and the number of casualties in Vietnam was at an all-time high. The Vietnam "war," technically a conflict, brought personal losses to families across our nation, adding to the overwhelming burden of grief. I strongly believe that unresolved grief is a core issue of PTSD and is currently at epidemic proportion in America.

The stage for our generation was set: the men and women who went to Vietnam thought they were standing for the values our forefathers taught us—truth, justice, and liberty—just as I did.

By 1968, many Americans believed our government was lying to us, not only about the presidential assassination, but also about the war. The protests grew into riots and violence in our city streets.

People wanting peace instead turned their wrath on our soldiers in Vietnam, which distracted them from holding the government accountable.

When returning home from the war, many were actually spit upon as they stepped foot on American soil. Sadly, some widows of the war also received hateful and threatening phone calls from people who cried "peace."

The political giants of that era slithered by while frustrated citizens and unappreciated soldiers became each other's enemy. We lost our country and our lives while our government sacrificed our young people for political and financial gain.

Bruce died in 1968 when the war was hot in Vietnam and America.

Our relationship began and ended in the spring of our lives, before callousness and desensitization seized our hearts.

Sacred Shadow, Sacred Ground

Entrance to *Phu Loc 6*

U.S. Marines descend into "Arizona Territory," the area where Bruce fought.

— Photos courtesy of Daniel Wiegmann.

Ambush Near Liberty Bridge
September 11, 1968

Sacred Shadow, Sacred Ground

> *"You think you are growing up fast, wait until you see boys go out on patrol and a few hours later you see men walk past you, because of what they have been through in the past hour or two. It isn't right to grow up that way... I guess your old hubby is growing up pretty fast over here Glen, anyway I feel a lot differently than when I left the United States."*
>
> — August 28, 1968

Like the other boys in Fox 2/5, Bruce became a man overnight. Early in August, just before Bruce had arrived, Fox 2/5 suffered a friendly napalm attack that wounded or killed most of 2nd Platoon.

It didn't take long for the Marines to get terrible blisters on their feet, and skin that would peel off when they were finally able to take off their boots. They spent days at a time in the fields, tromping around in thick bush and wet rice paddies.

It rained a lot and they were subjected to temperatures that reached into the 130's. Depending on the time of year, nights could also get very cold.

They had boils on their bodies and infected sores on their arms from scratches and insect bites. They wore the same torn, sweat-drenched and sometimes blood-soaked, clothing that often carried the stench of burnt flesh.

At first they bonded, until they saw one too many of their friends blown apart or burned beyond recognition. They quickly learned to distance themselves. Sometimes their friends bled to death in their arms.

Some days they were hungry because of lack of supplies. Then there were the days of major battles. The sounds

Ambush Near Liberty Bridge

of wounded men crying, screaming and raging could be heard through the noise of bombs blasting, guns firing, and grenades exploding.

They witnessed atrocities of war we don't want to think, hear or talk about. Many experienced survivor's guilt: "Why did I get to live while my brother beside me died?"

I've learned that this was Bruce's reality. These were the things he saw that he tried to protect me from knowing.

"Honey, I don't want you to worry about me and for that reason I haven't told you anything about what I'm doing over here..."
— August 26, 1968

"Honey, in one of your letters you ask what I did from day to day. I didn't go into detail because I don't want you to worry needlessly..."
— September 3, 1968

Area at *Phu Loc* 6 where the bodies of Bruce and the others were brought after the ambush.

Tanks on the "red" road to *An Hoa*. This is the road where Bruce and others died. Most likely, it is not the actual location.

— Photos courtesy of Daniel Wiegmann.

Ambush Near Liberty Bridge

On the day of the ambush, Bruce found time to write a letter to me and included a page of poems taken from a military magazine. I suppose he thought throughout most of the day that he would be doing something other than setting up an ambush site that night.

Platoons rotated every three to four days and it was time for 1st Platoon to take its rotation for ambush. It was getting late when Capt. Brown changed the orders and sent 2nd Platoon to set up ambush sites instead of 1st Platoon.

Two ammunition trucks got to the river too late to cross, so they had to be guarded throughout the night. Capt. Brown sent 1st Platoon across the river to guard the important cargo while 3rd Platoon remained close to the hill.

There are three squads in a platoon. Each squad consists of around 14 men, depending on the number of casualties and how fast they were replaced. One Marine reported that his platoon normally ran about 35 men, but at one time was down to eight because of heavy casualties.

Two squads left the compound within minutes of each other, while the third stayed close to the base to provide it with additional support.

Bruce and the others hurriedly finished eating their "B" Rations, and were the first squad out, which meant they would go the farthest from the compound. With only about 20 minutes left before nightfall, the 14 men moved quickly along the "Red Road" to *An Hoa*, which was lined with marshes and rice paddies. The road was called "red" because of the color of the soil.

"Ski" was Bruce's squad leader, a more experienced

Marine, who had recently returned from R&R. Cpl. Blount led the following squad. Dennis Cadigan was the "B" machine gunner who normally went with Ski's squad. However, on this particular night, Ski had given Jerry Evans, the "A" machine gunner, the opportunity to go with his squad. Being good friends, Jerry and Dennis had no problem with the switch because they were all leaving the compound anyway. Ken Murray was also in Blount's squad that night, as was Bill Martell and J. D. Moore.

Fox Co. had been setting up ambush sites along this stretch of road for several weeks. They had suffered losses of one or two men at a time to booby traps and mines, but didn't have many enemy sighting or contact. One of their jobs was to keep the road clear of land mines so convoys of supply trucks could travel from the *Song Tu Bon* river crossing to *An Hoa* without getting blown up.

According to one Marine, the smart way to set up an ambush was to go out while it was still light, set up, then move after dark, leaving the enemy a false position. However, on this night, the men left much later than they usually did.

Bruce's squad was out about 15 minutes when Blount's squad reached the bend in the road where a large tree stood as a familiar land marker. An old Vietnamese man came from nowhere babbling excitedly. Since none of the soldiers in Blount's squad spoke Vietnamese, they tried to have him talk to Capt. Brown by radio.

It didn't work.

The Vietnamese man did not want to talk into the radio. Capt. Brown could not make sense out of what he could not hear, so he told Blount to finish setting up.

It was at that moment the attack on Ski's squad took place. One Marine reports that both squads were taking fire, which kept Blount's squad in their position and unable to fire in the direction of the ambush for fear they would hit their own men.

Bruce, along with the others, was caught in a horseshoe ambush. The enemy circled in behind them and cut them off and killed them from behind and sides.

Ski turned and fired his gun at the enemy. Another Marine dropped and fired at the enemy. Two Marines ran to take cover in the bush, four were wounded, and Bruce Carter, Jerry Evans, Fred Spina, Frank Vallone, Bruce Crabb, Billy Joe Scott and George William Mc Gee were killed.

All reports I've found say they died quickly. Several, including Bruce, were shot in the head.

The wounded were screaming. Cadigan and the other men in Blount's squad fired at the enemy and called for support from the compound. He became enraged and continued to shoot until the barrel of his gun glowed from the heat.

The old man who tried to warn them had disappeared.

Within minutes, two tanks from the compound along with 3rd Platoon were on their way. Cadigan and the others fell in behind the M-55 tanks and within about ten minutes the rescue squads were at the ambush site.

Across the river, Eugene Caster, who was in Hotel 2/5, had just tucked in for the night. "They told us we would be safe, we could sleep in and have a late breakfast in the morning."

Skin peeled from Caster's feet as he took his boots off. He had fallen asleep and it was sometime after 7 p.m. when all chaos broke loose. He was abruptly awakened by the fire fight across the river.

"We were told to saddle up," Caster said.

Half conscious, he pulled on two different sized boots and was on his way. At first he thought they were going to the ambush site to rescue the men. Instead, they crossed over to provide cover in other areas while 3rd Platoon of Fox Co. went in to pull out their wounded and dead.

From where he was during the initial ambush, Eugene could see tracers from the guns, along with a white phosphorus flare that lit up the sky.

"I could see movement," Caster said. "The enemy was taking things off the bodies. You know, like dog tags, guns, or whatever they could get.

"It was a moment of terror that came across the radio. I could hear them yelling and screaming until it was over. The last thing I heard was someone saying, 'Please tell my mom...'"

When Cadigan and the others arrived on the scene, Ski seemed to be in shock and was disoriented. He saw Ski turn a body over. It had three gunshot wounds in the head and was burned black because a bullet had hit his (white phosphorus) flare. He turned the body back and started throwing up on the road.

Cadigan recognized the man as his friend.

Enraged, he began screaming, "You mother f_ _ kers! You, mother f_ _ kers!" as he fired his gun into the bush. The words "He's dead, he's dead, it could have been me," raced through his mind. His feelings were torn. He was upset because he lost his buddy and felt guilty for being glad he wasn't the one dead in the road.

Blount's squad helped to load the wounded on one tank and the dead were stacked on the other for transport back to the compound.

Cadigan and most of the first and second squads of 2nd Platoon stayed in their bunkers the rest of that night.

The cold night intensified the chill in their souls. Their torn uniforms were covered with blood, sweat and tears. They hovered in the darkness with many mixed emotions including grief, anger, fear and guilt. They listened to sounds of the wounded screaming and yelling.

At about 0200, choppers from *Da Nang* evacuated the wounded. Shortly thereafter, Capt. Brown, overwrought with anger, left with the rest of 3rd Platoon, along with the two tanks, and went back to the ambush site to see if they could locate the enemy.

About 0400, Caster came out of the trench. He needed to stand up and walk around and get some water. It was just getting light enough to see.

"I see the pile of Marines about 100 ft. away," Caster recalled. "I gravitated toward them."

"It was surreal."

He felt a quiet intrigue pull him closer so he could look at their faces. "It was the first time I witnessed this many casualties at one time, I had to look at them."

> "They looked united...a real brotherhood. There is a black man on top, entangled with a brown man, entangled with a guy with red hair—all were laid face up. Blood was running down, coagulated, mixed all together. I realized we were all the same. These were all my brothers."
>
> — Eugene Caster

"Then I became concerned because of flies...I didn't like how the Marines had been laid in a pile. I went to my corporal and complained. I mean, we always treat our fallen brothers with the greatest respect. Why were they in a pile? I was told it wasn't a matter of respect but a matter of circumstance.

"It was hard to realize they were expendable.

"Until now, going out on ambush was exhilarating. It felt good at ambush site. No one knew where you were, hopefully we could lay there and nothing would happen.

"It was like a cat and mouse game. It went back and forth, they would attack, we would attack.

"Until now we called them 'gooks', I don't know what a 'gook' is, I could kill them like shooting rabbits, like a kid in Nebraska, until I took a prisoner who spoke English.

"Then I realized they were human beings. After I saw them as human beings I began to ask, 'What is this for? What's the plan for the war? When will this be over?'"

In the early morning Ken, along with other Marines from Blount's squad, came out of their bunkers.

Ken Murray remembers, "We were ordered to view the

bodies stacked together. We were ordered not to show emotion. We didn't really know what had happened to them. I saw the 'Mighty Mike' go by. It was like a funeral procession, only worse. They were stacked together. A Mighty Mike was like a flat bed vehicle about six feet long, four feet wide and about three feet off the ground on four wheels. I don't know why we were ordered to look at them other than they wanted us to get mad so we would want to retaliate.

"Our morale had been down. It was bad because of where the rounds had been placed. Mostly they had all been shot in the face. It was one of the worst sights I saw in the 19 months I was there. Like maybe they stood over them and shot them."

By the time Cadigan looked at his one friend's burned, twisted body, all but three had been placed in body bags. The others, covered with ponchos, had to wait until more body bags arrived with the medevac chopper. *We'll get them for you*, he thought.

At about 0630, 1st Platoon returned with the two ammo trucks they had guarded through the night. Around 0730, a chaplain flew in on a Huey from *An Hoa*, completed a memorial service, returned to the waiting chopper and flew away. At about 0815, 1st and 2nd Platoons left the compound to join the rest of Fox Co. located near the tree at the curve in the road.

One of the Marines told me that when the chopper came to transport Bruce and the other six who died with him to *Da Nang*, "A private had a Jew's Harp, he stood on the bunker and played the 'Star Spangled Banner' and 'Amazing Grace' as they loaded the men onto the chopper."

Meanwhile, Fox Company continued their search and located the enemy. They wanted to attack but were given orders to wait. Within a few minutes another friend of Dennis Cadigan was shot. His friend was swearing and crying at the same time as he applied a bandage to his wounded leg. He was again overtaken with rage.

He grabbed his machine gun and started shooting while ignoring the radio handset, from which someone was telling them to "Hold your fire!"

Dennis said later, "I just 'frigging' ignored them!"

Minutes later a F-4 "Phantom" aircraft dropped bombs and fired its 20mm cannon on the enemy. By the time Cadigan's friend was picked up by the medevac chopper, 2nd and 3rd Platoons entered the hamlet of *Phu Loc* (3) where the firing came from the night before. The men were angry and explosive.

After interrogating several Vietnamese, Cadigan watched the same two tanks that carried their wounded and dead Marines the night before, run over and destroy the ten remaining hooches in which the Vietnamese lived.

That night lives changed. For some it became a natural and good feeling to kill the enemy in retaliation for killing their friends. Many traumatized Marines with survivor's guilt digging into their hearts acquired the "lust for enemy blood."

A few days later the ripple effect of that traumatic event was shared by the families of the seven who died.

Those moments, those few hellacious moments, altered the course of all our lives.

Missing Links

Threads of research
wove the scene
where Bruce was ambushed
with six other Marines.
I didn't know then
how they fell
or never dreamed
I'd be the one to tell.
Persistence beckoned that I try
to find the comrades with them
when they died.
I need to know what happened then,
so I can put away
the pain within.

Sacred Shadow, Sacred Ground

God, I just don't know what else to do.

All my leads and ideas on how to find anyone who may have known Bruce had been exhausted. In one last attempt I literally spent the night surfing the World Wide Web and posting messages on every site I could think of that might lead to someone who knew Bruce. As the light left the computer screen I thought, *That's it. I've done all I can, and all I know how to do.* My heart sank as I thought, *Maybe there's just no one left who remembers Bruce.*

Two days later I received an E-mail notification that I had a response to the query I had placed on a veterans website. I contacted the site and collected the message from Eugene Caster. He told me he was stunned to see my words on an Internet site, one that he had never visited before. We corresponded by E-mail until we were sure we were talking about the same battle that took place near Liberty Bridge. Several days passed before I had the courage to call him.

We talked for a long time, but I mostly listened as he shared what happened that night from his vantage point.

Eugene did not know Bruce personally but he gave me answers to many questions. He confirmed that Bruce was not alone when he died and that he and the others had died instantly.

As he described the scene of the seven bodies, and how their blood mixed together my throat tightened. He was crying and tears silently ran down my face.

I thought, *That's it! That's the sacred ground in the title of my book!*

The title had come to me months before during meditation. I hadn't known where the sacred ground was until that moment. It could have been the wall in Washington, D.C. or Bruce's grave site, but I didn't know it was the ground they bled upon.

It was as if their blood had sanctified the ground. They were blood brothers. That's why I have to find their families. We are all part of a large extended family.

As Eugene continued, he told me how that moment in 1968 had been a spiritual life-changing event for him. He vowed that if he was the one to return home, he would not let people forget.

We were both aware of God's presence. I shared with Eugene that there have been many times during the process of writing of this book that I've said, "It's a 'God Thing'."

Three decades ago, while thousands of miles away, he stood on the sacred ground of my book and became a messenger. This was another time my spirit quieted as I listened to the voice on the other end of the phone.

While he talked, my eyes were closed and I could see myself picking up an old rusty object. *What is it? Looks like a link to a chain. It is. My God, it's the missing link to the broken chain of my life.*

Because of the nature of the subject, Eugene expressed concern that he was giving me too much information. I didn't go into detail, but I told him that by sharing his story he had helped me to find the missing link.

His voice was compassionate and strong. He was articulate and easy to listen to. I felt a spiritual connection.

Sacred Shadow, Sacred Ground

"You have to tell this story," Eugene encouraged me, "it is bigger than you." He was the second to mention the "O" word. "Oprah." That meant exposure, national exposure. My anxiety peaked but I was able to laugh it off. *Yeah, right, Oprah.* It has become a private joke because the first time it was mentioned it scared me so bad I stopped writing for two weeks.

I had been a reluctant warrior until our discussion. I complained because the subject brought gut-wrenching pain. I bled emotional blood and cried toxic tears as I opened the wounds and dragged myself through the tunnel of unresolved grief.

During my conversation with Eugene, I began to sense a transformation. My reluctance disappeared and I realized that the word "shadows" in the title of my book represented the sacred part of myself that had covered my pain. As I came into the light of understanding, I began to see that my book was not my book at all. It was bigger than me. It was no longer a hardship I felt, but a sense of honor and privilege to be the one to tell this story.

I too have become a messenger.

I had set aside the hope of finding someone who could personally remember Bruce, and finished writing the chapter on the Ambush. I knew how Bruce had died, and understood more about how he lived the last days of his life. That would have to be enough.

Then, by snail mail, I received a letter from Chris Brown. Chris has helped me, along with many other people, connect with family and friends.

The roster he enclosed listed the names of Fox Company Marines. The 60 names that had been highlighted were the names of those known to be in the area around Liberty Bridge the night Bruce was killed.

My mind struggled, *What are the odds anyone will remember Bruce? Sixty names, that's a potential for sixty more gruesome war stories. That's a lot of work just to be disappointed again. However, if I don't contact everyone on this list, I'll never know. I have to follow the trail.*

Chris wrote an introductory paragraph for me to include in a letter. His extra effort was the decisive point and encouraged me to continue my search.

As I placed each letter in a hand-addressed envelope, I felt like I was being an obedient servant to a higher power.

I put my return address sticker on the top left corner and paused to say a prayer.

Sixty letters, sixty prayers.

A few months earlier I may have prayed something like, *Please God, let one of these guys remember Bruce. Please!* Instead of the childlike begging, I asked God to bless the one whose name was on the envelope.

Two days after mailing the letter, I received my first response from Steve Nolley, who happens to live in my state. His voice seemed a little unsure when we first began to talk. "We went through training together. I remember

Sacred Shadow, Sacred Ground

when he showed me your picture. We went in country together, we were close. I was the one who was able to identify him."

The next day I received another phone call from Don, who also trained with Bruce. "I remember we teased him when he got married".

With the first two replies, I felt a sense of completion: someone who had been on the battlefield with Bruce still remembered.

I received several other responses from Marines who did not remember him personally; however, they felt compelled to respond to my inquiry. In each case, they provided other links to my chain of healing.

The connections are making me stronger. I am becoming whole again.

In Memory

PFC Bruce Landon Carter
PFC Bruce Wayne Crabb
PFC Jerry Brian Evans
PFC George William Mc Gee
PFC Billy Joe Scott
LCPL Fred Concetto Spina
PFC Frank Vallone

THE SEVEN

Sacred Shadow, Sacred Ground

The Seven

PFC Bruce Landon Carter
1950 - 1968

United States Marine Corps
Born: June 2, 1950
Home of Record: Milton-Freewater, Oregon
Marital Status: Married
Start of Tour: Tuesday, August 13, 1968
KIA: September 11, 1968
Quang Nam Province,
South Vietnam
Age at Death: 18
Buried: Enterprise, Oregon

Bruce's older sister Mary and her husband Ed helped raise Bruce after his father disappeared when he was just a child. "He was like a son to us."

Mary, Ed and I were able to share memories of Bruce, the sweet child, the brother and the husband for the first time in 2004.

They told me what he was like when he was just a little boy.

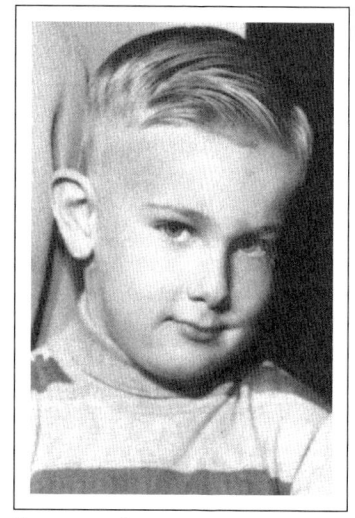

Bruce at age 3.

"When he was about three years old, he lived on a farm outside Enterprise, Oregon.

"One day he and his dog came up missing.

"It was a large area to cover. People from town came out to help with the search."

As it got dark his mother became even more worried and when the dog they affectionately called 'Spud Murphy' came home without Bruce, she was frantic.

"About an hour or two later, Bruce showed up, wondering what all the commotion was about. He said, he was just out looking over the farm. He wanted to see what it looked like at night. He said Spud Murphy got tired, but he didn't, and that's why the dog came home without him."

Even at three he was adventurous!

"The most rebellious thing he ever did was to get a "Mohawk" haircut when he was in high school. He thought Mom would really be mad, but she figured he'd get tired of it soon enough. He did. It wasn't long until he was wearing a cap. He even wore it under his football helmet to try to cover it up."

He loved sports and was smart. He quit school when he was 17 to join the Marines.

He had a close relationship with his mother who died only six months before Bruce was killed.

Bruce is remembered by friends and family as kind, considerate and having an all-around. upstanding character. He was loyal to family, friends and country. He is still missed.

An American and a Christian Flag were donated in his memory to the Assembly of God church, where he was married and baptized.

Vietnam Veterans Memorial
Panel 44 W – Row 021

Sacred Shadow, Sacred Ground

The Seven

PFC Bruce Wayne Crabb
1948 - 1968

United States Marine Corps

Born: September 26, 1948
Home of Record: Milwaukee, Wisconsin
Marital Status: Single
Start of Tour: Monday, August 12, 1968
KIA: September 11, 1968
Quang Nam Province, South Vietnam
Age at Death: 19
Buried: Glen Haven, Ohio

Sacred Shadow, Sacred Ground

"It's been over 33 years and the pain of your death is still very heavy. I really miss you, little brother. Mom grieved 30 years, 178 days. She always did look forward to being with you. I've never stopped missing you, and now I pray for you both."

— Bob Crabb (brother)

One more day and I would have been in Vietnam one month. Fifteen more days and I would have turned 20 years old. I was planning to marry my childhood sweetheart when I came home, the girl I had gone with since the seventh grade.

I would have been able to spend more time getting to know my brother. My mother would not have had to grieve and live the agony of losing a son.

I don't know what I could have become, had I lived.

— Photos on previous pages courtesy of Bob Crabb

Vietnam Veterans Memorial
Panel 44 W – Row 023

Sacred Shadow, Sacred Ground

PFC Jerry Brian Evans
1948 - 1968

United States Marine Corps

     Born: November 6, 1948
Home of Record: Wurtsboro, New York
 Marital Status: Single
  Start of Tour: Wednesday, August 14, 1968
      KIA: September 11, 1968
        Quang Nam Province, South Vietnam
  Age at Death: 19
    Buried: Sylvan Cemetery, Wurtsboro, New York

Sacred Shadow, Sacred Ground

Jerry Evans (left) and his cousin James Arnott

All I ever wanted to do was play Army or Cowboys and Indians. It was enough to imagine our manhood, measuring it in terms of acted heroism, valor and strength.

Our play had a great effect on our development. Maybe it was our parents' generation and their involvement in World War II that helped shape our sense of duty and rampant militarism.

Little did we realize that in six or seven short years we would trade the dirt-bomb hand grenades and foxholes for M-16s, C-rations and jungle...for real.

— From a work in progress by James Arnott

Jerry is remembered and missed by family and friends. Each year a small scholarship is given in his honor to a local high school senior.

As of 2004, his parents continue to live in the small community of Wurtsboro, New York. His cousin's son, Jim Arnott Jr., just returned from the war in Iraq.

Each year his friend, Jim Carney, visits the Vietnam memorial and places a remembrance in his honor.

Jerry Evans, H.S. senior

One of the most painful messages I received from my new extended family was that one week before Jerry's body arrived home from Vietnam, his younger sister, Jennifer, was killed in a car accident.

Jerry's parents buried two of their three children side by side at the same time.

— Photos courtesy of James Arnott & James Carney

Vietnam Veterans Memorial
Panel 44 W – Row 023

Sacred Shadow, Sacred Ground

The Seven

PFC George William Mc Gee
1950 - 1968

> We honor your memory as one of the seven.
> Your ultimate sacrifice will not be forgotten.
> May your soul rest in peace.

United States Marine Corps
Born: February 3, 1950
Home of Record: Oklahoma City, Oklahoma
Marital Status: Single
Start of Tour: Thursday, May 16, 1968
KIA: September 11, 1968
Quang Nam Province,
South Vietnam
Age at Death: 18
Buried: Unknown

Attempts to locate George's family or friends have been unsuccessful to date.

Vietnam Veterans Memorial
Panel 44 W – Row 028

Sacred Shadow, Sacred Ground

The Seven

PFC Billy Joe Scott
1947 - 1968

> We honor your memory as one of the seven. Your ultimate sacrifice will not be forgotten. May your soul rest in peace.

United States Marine Corps
Born: December 10, 1947
Home of Record: Cincinnati, Ohio
Marital Status: Single
Start of Tour: Sunday, June 23, 1968
KIA: September 11, 1968
Quang Nam Province, South Vietnam
Age at Death: 20
Buried: Unknown

Attempts to locate Billy Joe's family or friends have been unsuccessful to date.

Vietnam Veterans Memorial
Panel 44W – Row 029

Sacred Shadow, Sacred Ground

LCPL Fred Concetto Spina
1949 - 1968

United States Marine Corps

Born: August 6, 1949
Home of Record: Woodbury, New Jersey
Marital Status: Single
Start of Tour: Tuesday, December 19, 1967
KIA: September 11, 1968
 Quang Nam Province,
 South Vietnam
Age at Death: 19
Buried: St. Joseph's Cemetery,
 Swedesboro, New Jersey

Sacred Shadow, Sacred Ground

Fred Spina at age 1

A mother can see through the military uniform. The heart grieves for the creation she carried within her womb. She mourns the loss of innocence and life of the child she nurtured from infancy.

"September 11 used to be our day. We carried it with us since 1968. Now, so many people mourn on that day. Fred was born and he died on historical days. August 6, was when they dropped the bomb in Japan. And now September 11 is a historical day.

"Fred grew up a very clean-cut young man who never got into trouble. As far back as a young teen, Fred knew he was going to be a Marine. Everything he did was based on the military. He went into the Marines two weeks after graduation from high school.

"But Fred got a lot out of life. He excelled in everything he did. He became a champion wrestler, played baseball and became a pitcher and was a switch hitter.

"We dedicated a flag pole in his honor, where the flag flies day and night in front of our church.

"We will always love and honor him."

— Francis Spina, Fred's mother
Photo courtesy of Francis Spina

The Seven

While in Vietnam, Fred was wounded when a booby trap exploded. Only two days later, he was one of several in Fox Company burned by the friendly napalm attack mentioned in the "Ambushed" chapter. He was able to call home via a Ham radio operator one month before he died. That was the last time his mother heard from him.

In one of the last letters Francis Spina received from her son, he expressed his faith in God.

"...It's Sunday morning now and I went to church and received Communion. For some reason, I feel really clean. I don't mean physically, but mentally. Church really means a lot to me out here. I guess because being out in the bush makes me feel a lot closer to God. I really never understood church or the meaning of prayer until now. I guess the bush makes a guy grow up real fast, he has to or he won't survive. He also has to believe in God to see him through this. If not, again he won't survive. I believe in God."

— Letter printed by permission from Francis Spina
Previously published in *They Were Ours* by John Campbell

Vietnam Veterans Memorial
Panel 44W – Row 031

Sacred Shadow, Sacred Ground

PFC Frank Vallone
1949 - 1968

United States Marine Corps

Born:	April 4, 1949
Home of Record:	New York City, New York
Marital Status:	Single
Start of Tour:	Sunday, July 7, 1968
KIA:	September 11, 1968 Quang Nam Province, South Vietnam
Age at Death:	19
Buried:	Long Island National Cemetery

Sacred Shadow, Sacred Ground

Frank grew up in Manhattan's Little Italy. He was big brother and father figure to a sister and two younger brothers after his parents separated. Frank was quick to accept responsibility and quit school early to work at a local butcher shop.

"He helped support the family by helping mom with the bills and he made sure there were presents for us under the Christmas tree. Frank was the kind of brother any kid would want. He checked out all the guys who I dated, and made sure my mini dresses weren't too mini. Everyone loved him. He was the kind of guy that moms would hope their daughters would bring home to meet the family.

"When everyone was being drafted into the Army, Frank decided that if he had to go into the service he wanted to go with the best, the Marines.

"My mother signed for him to go because he was not yet 18. I think she always regretted signing for him but it is what he wanted."

Frank trained at Paris Island and the family went to his graduation.

"His chest was just bursting with pride. We were all so proud of him and I thought my big brother was the handsomest Marine there.

"There was a kindness about him that just seemed to come so naturally from him. He was the kind of kid who helped little old ladies cross the street.

"After he died, the people of the neighborhood put a plaque on the church rectory doors. People still talk about him.

The Seven

Frank (center) with friends.

"Frank lived for peace and love and just being happy. He was a kind and wonderful spirit. At a time when drugs and free sex was the norm, my brother was thinking about doing his part for his country, and he was proud to be part of the best."

There is not a day that goes by that I don't think of you. I talk to you and laugh with you as though you are still here and it makes me feel good, because I know you can hear me and see me. I Love You so much Frank, and one day I will get to spend eternity with you, and then we'll catch up on things.

I love you.

Your sister, Roseann

Posted on www.virtualwall.org.
Printed by permission. Photos courtesy of Roseann Oliveri

Vietnam Veterans Memorial
Panel 44W – Row 032

WELCOME HOME

Sacred Shadow, Sacred Ground

Raindrops puddled on the rooftop next door as I peered out my hotel window. My four-day trip to Washington, D. C. was ending. I prepared to go to the granite wall one more time before leaving.

Along with new friends, I had made the three-block walk from my hotel to the Vietnam Veterans Memorial enough times to familiarize myself with the area.

It was cold and dark the first time I went to the wall. The small lights spaced along the bottom did not seem adequate for such a great monument. The darkness made visitors look like shadow people wandering in the night. My day visits had been filled with a lot of people and November sunshine. My last visit on this trip would be another of my "I gotta walk it by myself" moments.

Each day, we passed the Department of State building, where guards blocked entrances and both ends of the street. The cement barriers represented the signs of our times. Placed on the outside of the curb, they made it more difficult for both foot and automobile traffic. Guards had guns and dogs which searched vehicles that arrived at the entrances of the State building.

We could not forget that we were in the middle of another war. Iraq and terrorists were on our minds. Police officers looked cautious as we passed.

It was all new to me, and my photographic ambitions caused me to point my camera in their direction. Immediately the officer came from behind the black SUV. It reminded me of last summer when a bull was rounded up in my front yard and herded toward me. I froze. The man in uniform was far enough away he could

Welcome Home

not have heard my camera release. However, I was sure he could see my finger press the button, and would mistake it as an act of defiance. His heightened sense of alertness withered as I quickly withdrew my photographic stance and left the area.

My camera had become like a weightless attachment of myself. However, it suddenly felt cumbersome as I prepared for my last journey to the wall. I placed Bruce's watch in my right pants pocket along with my wallet, and headed for the elevator, having left my camera behind. The long hallway lined with closed doors reminded me that the thousands of people who gathered yesterday to observe Veterans Day had gone home.

Cloud cover warned of its intent to spill more water, but for now it had stopped raining. Dressed for warmth, I felt confident as I stepped into the morning light. The city was just waking up and getting back to its normal flow.

Before my trip to D.C., I had prepared for an emotional, gut-wrenching reaction. It was interesting that I had not cried many tears nor felt Bruce's presence during this trip.

I wondered why. *Did I slip into denial and not allow my emotions to surface? Was I too distracted by new friends and the over powering sense of history to feel the loss of Bruce?*

Throughout my visit I soaked in the feelings of acceptance, extended family, and the familiarity that brought emotional intimacy. I had found a sense of community, brother and sisterhood. I was out of my isolation, and it felt good.

But wasn't I supposed to meet Bruce at the wall? After all,

Sacred Shadow, Sacred Ground

I had traveled clear across the United States to deal with the Wall and all that it stands for.

Would this last part of my journey cause my tears to flow like they have so many times before? It was time to allow my heart to open and face the wall without the shelter of my camera lens.

The quiet assurance of God's presence settled my heart from any fear of being alone in the big city. I was ready to continue my pilgrimage. Staying open to my present reality was of the utmost importance. I did not want to lose focus. The meeting my heart beckoned me to attend was only moments away. I would stand in front of the dark granite wall and confront whatever awaited.

My overwhelming sense of belonging was a comfort as I placed one foot in front of the other on wet paved ground. As I entered the National Mall, I surveyed my surroundings and saw one woman jogger.

The imposing splendor of the Washington monument captured my attention as the misty morning light lifted its veil. It was a photographer's "fringe benefit," one of those experiences that you can only capture in your heart, not on film. I paused to breathe in the beauty of the scene and accept the magnificent power I felt all around me.

Then I turned, and from the east side, entered what felt like an arranged private showing of a great monument.

My feet touched the sacred ground as I slowed my pace and walked reverently by thousands of names, just to get to one.

"How many deaths does it take before we know too

many people have died?" The words to Bob Dylan's song, "Blowin' In The Wind," haunted me until I gave the answer.

One, it only takes one, if that one is the person that you love.

There was not another person in sight. Having the famous wall to myself felt like it had been arranged by my God. Along the bottom of the wall stood flowers, medals, poems, wreaths, and even a doll, as gifts of remembrance. The space was mine.

I've done everything visitors normally do at the wall. Several times I completed the walk from one end of the wall to the other, passing by the more than 58,000 names.

I took photographs and touched the etching of Bruce's name. I also touched the names of the Marine brothers who died with him. I had placed my hand on the wall and felt the heat it captured from the sun. I visited at night when it was cold and visitors looked like ghost shadows moving about. One time a stranger stopped and offered to take my picture with my new friends as we stood in front of the names that brought us together. I observed people as they walked their own journeys. A friend did Bruce's name rubbing for me. People were courteous and kind. Almost everyone carried a camera.

They talked quietly, if they talked at all. Tourists seemed to meander their way through the gathering while others met with hugs, tears, and laughter. They shared stories as brothers and sisters do. Like myself, many were there for the first time while others returned and attended yearly reunions.

I overheard a small boy excitedly ask his mother, "Did

he fight in the war?" His eyes filled with awe as if he were looking at a bigger-than-life living monument. At first I thought he was talking about a World War II veteran. Then I turned to see the man, dressed in unmatched Vietnam-era clothing, with an unshaven face and long gray hair. I smiled to myself thinking that sometimes I forget how old we have become.

Throughout the day I watched as people would point to a name on the wall and wait for someone to snap a photograph. *Why? Is it a tourist thing?* I wondered to myself, *What significance does that pose have, and why do so many people do it?*

Then, it was my turn to take my place beside Bruce's name. As I held my hand close to the etched letters I felt a sense of belonging. For the first time I understood that I am a "part of" the living history of the famous wall, not merely a visitor or an observer. My friend snapped the shutter that documented my presence at the historic Vietnam Veterans Memorial and I felt as though I had come home.

For more than 30 years I had gone from job to job, relationship to relationship, feeling a heavy sense of failure and shame. I was not able to establish an identity. When people would ask me what I did for a living, what answer could I give them? The truthful answer would have been,

I spend my time doing whatever it takes to survive.

For the first time in three decades I found a place where I felt that—*I really belong.*

Many veterans greeted one another with the words,

"Welcome home." I longed for someone to say them to me because I felt like I had come home too.

Volunteers with yellow caps helped guests locate names. Name-rubbings on a paper that has Vietnam Veteran Memorial across the top are often sent to people who cannot travel to D. C. The valuable service of the yellow cap volunteers help people from all over the world to locate the name of their loved one.

Veterans seemed to be easier to identify than widows and other family members. Perhaps it was the caps and jackets with patches and logos attached to them that helped them identify each other. I didn't see any women wearing a patch or shirt that said, "Widow." I didn't see anyone wearing the words, "sons" or "daughters," nor "mother" or "father." I know the *Sons and Daughters* organization was represented because I saw the wreath they left. If there was a wreath from the "Widows of War," I had missed it.

I began to search for members of Bruce's company by reading patches, looking at logos and asking Marines if they had seen anyone from Fox Company. I found no one.

One Marine suggested that I wear a shirt with "Widow" written across it. For most of my life I had lived in emotional isolation and seclusion. Yet, when this stranger suggested I label myself with the word I had avoided for over 30 years, I felt as if it was an invitation to join the family. As I walked away he said, "Welcome home."

Next time I will wear a garment that will acknowledge

the part of my identity that belongs to the wall.

It felt surreal to be where Bruce joined thousands in documenting a tragic part of our history.

My sense of belonging was intense. This was the most comfortable place in the world for me to be. My thoughts rambled. *I could move here so I could volunteer at the wall and walk this path every day. No, wait, it's only like this right now because people have come from all over the States.*

I visualized an old woman maintaining a daily vigil in front of the wall. I realized it was me. The "at home" feeling tightened its grip as it tried to keep me captive in it's comfort. Instead I released it. *I can't live here, I can't make the wall my life. This is a family reunion; I can come back home to visit, but I can't move in.*

Sometimes the healing process brings us to a place that is too painful, or to a place so comfortable, that we choose to abandon our journey.

It was time to put aside the memories I had gathered and say my last good-bye on this, my first quest, to Washington, D. C. and the Vietnam Veterans Memorial.

My hand came from my pocket and wiped the moisture from the morning rain off his name. *Why don't I feel your presence Bruce?* I pulled the red rose I brought from the hotel from inside my jacket and knelt to place it beside the picture at the bottom of the wall. His watch was in my hand and for a moment I thought of leaving it beside the rose. Instead, I slid it back into my pocket.

In the short time I was there, it had become a ritual to complete the walk of the wall. Knowing that time was growing short I turned and headed to the end where the

Welcome Home

west side begins. I wasn't thinking about completing the circle, I just felt drawn to walk to the end before leaving.

This isn't good-bye is it? It's only, "So long, I'll come back again when my work is finished, next year, yeah, next year." I don't understand it all now, but I will when I have time to think about it. Like, why am I walking to the end of the wall?

As I started back to Bruce's name, a man who had also come from the east side approached. We greeted one another and he told me he was a Veteran. I introduced myself as a widow. He shook my hand and said he was sorry for my loss. He asked to see Bruce's name. We walked a few feet, and I listened as the man with the friendly face and soft hand continued to tell me his story.

Later, I couldn't recall what he had said, only that we were two people who met briefly and shared a special quiet moment by the wall. We had been able to tell each other of our loss and wish each other well. I wondered how his presence played into my special viewing of the wall. *Was he a messenger?* There are thousands and thousands of stories like his, and like mine. When he left I again had the space to myself.

The tip of my fingers found their way to Bruce's name one more time and I realized it was still dry from when I had wiped off the rain. *I don't know where you are Bruce, but you're not here. What did you do, stay in Oregon? I thought we were suppose to meet here.*

It's okay that you aren't here because this trip is not about good-bye is it. I'm not ready to say good-bye.

In quiet contemplation I knew I had done what I was supposed to do on this part of my journey. My heart was

127

at peace, I felt confident, centered, content and strong. *I will return* I thought, but for now my personal work here was finished. I was ready to walk away.

I felt God's presence watching over me.

I not only needed to remember Bruce, I needed to get in touch with the part of me that accompanied him to his grave. I needed to find the wounded self that wandered aimlessly, cloaked in the blackness of despondency until I was lost in barren land.

I not only lost Bruce, I lost who I was and who I could have become with Bruce in my life.

The majestic wall began to work its wonder. Touching the wall and seeing my reflection brought me face to face with that part of myself that had refused to go on living without him.

The rain slid down the granite face, *My God, it looks like teardrops seeping from the engraved names.*

I looked down the empty path and back at the wall. I felt the presence of the thousands who were there just yesterday, and I felt the tears of those who remained behind the wall.

It Was an Epiphany

My spirit's search for you
lost in grief
hoping
you will find your way
to your day
of reckoning.
I wait and beckon you—
touch my face,
find my name,
take your place
in history.
Reconnect
the parts
that died that day.
Tears are shed in sorrow
for those who walk away
with personal wars
unresolved
until yet another day.
My happy tears
are spent
on those who take the time
to come to remember
the days
When, we were all so young and innocent,
Before we died.

Sacred Shadow, Sacred Ground

It's You, It's Me

I looked into the wall of tears
and saw me standing there.
Inside, looking out,
Outside, looking In.
It's you,
It's me,
It's where I've been—
Inside granite.
I can't come out,
You can't come in.
But now we know
where we are.
I see you,
you see me.
I belong here,
You belong there,
No need to search
anymore.
My wandering soul
found it's way.
I touched your hand
As you touched mine.
I whispered,
"Welcome home."

Angels cry with joy, when even one lost soul comes home.

— Glenda Carter

VIETNAM VETERANS MEMORIAL
WASHINGTON, D.C.
NOVEMBER 2003

PHOTOGRAPHS BY GLENDA M. CARTER

Sacred Shadow, Sacred Ground

Vietnam Veterans Memorial

Sacred Shadow, Sacred Ground

Vietnam Veterans Memorial

Sacred Shadow, Sacred Ground

Vietnam Veterans Memorial

Sacred Shadow, Sacred Ground

Vietnam Veterans Memorial

Sacred Shadow, Sacred Ground

Vietnam Veterans Memorial

Sacred Shadow, Sacred Ground

Vietnam Veterans Memorial

"Then it was my turn to take my place beside Bruce's name...For the first time I understood that I am a "part of" the living history of the famous wall..."

— Photo by John Campbell

Sacred Shadow, Sacred Ground

"It was a divine intervention, I had the wall to myself."

LOST CHILD

Sacred Shadow, Sacred Ground

When I visited Bruce's sister for the first time in more than 15 years, she gave me this photo of Bruce taken when he was about three months old. I brought it home and stood it on my dresser where I could easily see it.

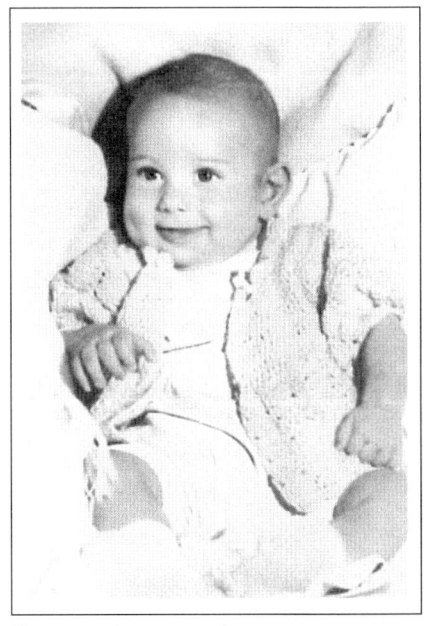

Bruce at three months

The innocent-looking, bright-eyed baby I saw in the picture made me wonder if that was what our child would have looked like. It began to represent the baby we never had.

I began to feel angry. Thirty-five-year-old anger marched its way from my gut.

I cried, I wanted to hit something or at least throw a few things. I did neither.

The tears rolled heavily down my cheeks as I sobbed.

It's not okay, it's not okay that Bruce died in Vietnam.

How dare our government sacrifice our young people for greed and power.

At the time of this writing we are at war in Iraq. Often, I hear a particular news broadcaster report on a casualty of the Iraq war. Each time he says, "He/she will be buried with FULL MILITARY HONORS." Again, I want to scream.

Don't they get it? FULL MILITARY HONORS does not take

Lost Child

the friggin' pain away.

As I looked at the picture, I felt how a mother must feel at the loss of a child, when that child is their innocent, bright-eyed beautiful baby. *It's not okay! It's just not okay.* I was talking aloud to myself. I realized I had not only lost Bruce, but I also lost the child we never had the opportunity to have.

I was angry with the politicians.

Our jails should be full. Full of protesters. I will not shut up any longer. I felt like Scarlet in *Gone With The Wind*, when she shook her fist and made a vow never to be hungry again.

I will not pretend it was okay for Bruce to have died in war by settling for "Full Military Honors." May lying politicians lose their teeth, may all their hair fall out, may they mess themselves in public.

I knew I needed to work off the toxic energy that kept surfacing. I got on my treadmill, then wrote some more. Still, by nightfall the anger hadn't subsided. I got on the treadmill again. Two hours later I needed another work out. I used my niece's *Total Gym*™ sitting in my living room until I became nauseated and feared I was pushing my overweight body into a heart attack.

It was as if a volcano had erupted and spewed its fiery poison from my being, toxic waste that I carried from the day Bruce was killed had just surfaced.

For the first time, I allowed myself to grieve as a mother, for the loss of a child.

Sacred Shadow, Sacred Ground

Memorial Day

Sacred Shadow, Sacred Ground

My mother and I drove the 80 miles to Enterprise Cemetery where Bruce is buried. This was the first trip we had made together to the cemetery in more than 30 years.

It was cloudy and pockets of rain poured on us as we left our own valley. The fields were as green as they get. The clouds hovered—whites and grays—patches of blue. The sun peaked through about halfway there and decided to stay out. I'd never seen the land more beautiful.

It was a peaceful drive and even my mother seemed content with moments of silence. We passed through Wallowa and talked about old friends we used to know who live there. It was graduation day, and as we drove past the school, we saw a man and his family whom we had been discussing. They wouldn't have recognized me, but one of the girls (now in her 30's) caught my glance. I think we knew each other. I waved.

Memorial Day

Enterprise is in the most beautiful valley I have ever seen. As we entered the cemetery I wanted to show my mother this view of the mountains you get only if you take the right path and allow your senses to work with you. Thus, I guided her through it, and as we turned the corner, I coached her to keep her eyes closed until just the right moment. The sun was out and clouds hung over the snow-topped Wallowa range. The sight of lilac bushes and the smell of freshly mown green grass added to the overall beauty of the scene.

We marveled at the greatness of the mountain as we went to Bruce's grave. The first thing I noticed was that there was not a flag. We placed the flowers we brought on his headstone. I helped my 81-year-old mother walk on the uneven ground. Since the wind was blowing and the temperature was cool, she didn't stand outside the car for long.

I didn't know who to contact about putting a flag out. I didn't have one but intended to see we put one on before leaving town. I told mom I wanted to drive around again so I could take a photograph of the road with the mountain behind. I started to turn to my right, but realized all the roads had been blocked so traffic would flow one direction. I drove back to the main entrance and we made our way around again.

There were several people in the cemetery; some were placing flowers, others had brought flags. I went on about my business and took a photograph of the road Bruce and I walked that I mentioned previously in my book. I waited until a white SUV moved off the path so

I could get a picture of it empty.

As I headed toward Bruce's grave for the second time I saw a red car pull up and stop across from where we had been. It was facing the wrong direction. As I spied a woman with a flag and some flowers, I thought to myself, *She looks like she will know something. I'll ask her as we go by.* As we drew closer, I realized this woman was at Bruce's grave placing a flag and flowers.

I didn't recognize her, but I was excited to think she may have known Bruce. *Who knows*, I thought, *maybe she's family or an old school friend.* I pulled beside her and asked her, "Are you related to Bruce?"

"No," she said, "I just watch over his grave."

She told me he had married some girl named__, and told me all she knew. I told her who I was and that I was Bruce's wife, and that since he had only been married once, he had not married that person (whom I happened to know, and knew she had never known Bruce either—that's another story for another time.).

"Just a minute, I'll park my car." Mom stayed in the car while I went back to talk with the woman, who told me her story.

She had been there the night before and saw they had forgotten to place a flag on Bruce's grave and a couple of others' in the cemetery, so she decided to bring one from home. She has several family members in the cemetery so she comes there often.

Every year on Memorial Day and Veterans Day, she and her two daughters made sure there were flowers and a flag on Bruce's grave. She had been doing this through the years I was not emotionally or physically able to do so.

She seemed a little put out that they had missed putting a flag on his grave. "I don't know why they missed his grave."

"I do," I said. "Forgive them, because if they had put the flag there, we would not be talking right now because you would not have come back to put out a flag. Have you thought about the timing? 'This is a God thing.'"

"Well," she said, "I was going to come around ten this morning." It was after 1 p.m.

She had been in the Marines. She lost the father of her first child in Vietnam. As she told me about it, tears ran down her face and mine. Neither of us spoke for a few moments.

I asked her what brought her to take care of Bruce's grave in the first place. Several things: she noticed there were never any flowers, that he was a Marine, and his age. She was young, too, when her child's father was killed in Vietnam. His family had taken him back East to bury.

They did not have anything to do with her or their granddaughter.

Marines are a tight extended family. They have a sense of duty that continues throughout the rest of their lives.

She also told me she is the mayor. So, here is the mayor and I standing beside Bruce's grave with the chill of the wind to our backs and tears running down our faces. I told her how messed up I had been and was not able to visit Bruce's grave for several years.

She said she will tell her daughters, and that they will be interested in hearing his story. I told her this is where

Sacred Shadow, Sacred Ground

I will one day be buried. She said she will tell her daughters, and not to worry because if she's gone, her daughters will watch over my site, also.

When I told Mom all of this on the way home, she said, "That's nice to know, because I was worried about who would do that with you buried clear over here away from the rest of the family." She also said in regard to this lady thinking Bruce's wife was someone else, "Well, I'm glad you cleared that up." Those who know my mother know how funny that is.

I don't know about you, but for me this was another case of Divine intervention. The timing amazes me. I certainly did not arrange this meeting and I don't believe in coincidence. I also know this meeting was not just for me to meet her, but was also for her to meet me. I learned I can share my story and talk about Bruce now without feeling I'm going to just die in my tracks. I know I've experienced a lot of healing.

I had always felt guilty because I had abandoned Bruce's memory and grave. Just to know this family cared enough to watch over his grave brings me comfort. I can see two small girls fussing over it every Memorial and Veteran Day. Wow.

I would like to meet them someday.

On the way home I saw a bird sitting on a fence post, looking out over the most beautiful, colorful landscape ever. "Mom, what do you think that bird is thinking about?" I was moved to silence and to seriousness. I wanted to say, "Mom, am I ready for what is going to happen with this book?"

Memorial Day

After dropping my mother off, I felt a little sad. I wished I had someone to share this story with. But how could I share this story? For me, it all felt like another "God Thing." There have been so many "God Things" during the process of writing this book, I stand amazed.

When I got to my house I called a friend and told her the story. I told her about the moment of seriousness. "You know, like when you fall in love and you have that emotional serious moment when you just know and it becomes the most real thing you've ever experienced? I had that with Bruce. Do you know what that feels like?"

She said, "No."

I am beginning to feel like this is what my whole life is about. This is why I lived. I am beginning to feel that I went through all the things I've gone through just so I can tell this story.

Sometimes I feel sad because I'm not in a relationship with someone I can come home to and share this stuff with. But then I remember a quote I read the other day.

"When all you have left is God, that is when you know that God is all you need." I don't know who wrote it.

Sacred Shadow, Sacred Ground

Finale

Sacred Shadow, Sacred Ground

The time for the grand finale of my life's work was drawing near. Just as I sat down to write, E-mails arrived, the phone rang, people who haven't written or called in a long time suddenly wanted my attention.

Fear made me pause and wallow in my inhibitions and insecurities. However, this particular journey through unresolved grief was coming to an end. I felt it in my gut, and in my attitude. I felt it in spite of my loss for words and my inability to go forward.

The mountains, with their jagged, snow-covered edges, symbolized the emotional terrain I still had to climb before I could utter the words, "It is finished."

I'd grown tired of hearing myself say, "When my book is finished, I can…"

At times I felt myself wanting to run and hide. I wanted it to be magically completed. I wanted to go out and play with friends in the sunshine and participate in life.

I had hoped to have had the manuscript in the final editor's hands by June 14. Instead, I agreed to work a week at my part-time job for the local newspaper. Part of me welcomed the distraction. However, as the week unfolded it felt like a week from Hell.

It was the week of the funeral for former President Ronald Reagan. Again, the country was in a state of mourning.

Finale

Scenes of the flag-draped casket triggered my memories of the 60's when President Kennedy was killed. Seeing Nancy Reagan mourn publicly for the love of her life triggered strong emotion. I stopped watching the news because of the repetitive coverage.

Monday, I began to feel my brain start shutting down as I inadvertently invaded a coworker's space. I became irritable as I tried to find a temporary sense of belonging.

By Wednesday my confidence wavered—I felt like I might be contracting *Alzheimer's*. I felt similar to when my PTSD was being triggered. It was severe enough to frighten me because I felt like the pathways in my brain were blocked. I could not think, remember or concentrate.

Feelings of shame and personal defeat overwhelmed me. *If I cannot keep my thoughts together to do this job, what can I do?* Memories of my inability to maintain focus frightened me.

I thought I had worked through all that, but here I was dealing with it again. I began to have serious doubts about being able to finish writing this book.

Wednesday, I printed a photograph of a man who was home from the war in Iraq, recovering from his wounds. It was called "Wounded," a reminder that we are at war.

That night when I turned on the television, uniformed pall bearers were taking Reagan's flag-draped casket into the rotunda of the Capitol building in Washington, D.C. Again, my mind flashed to the 60's.

When the service ended, I watched Vice President Cheney offer to walk Nancy Reagan to the casket. This being an election year, politicians must have been wondering how they can capitalize on this public event. Nancy responded as if his gesture was unplanned.

Gently stroking the casket with her hand, Mrs. Reagan affectionately laid her head against it; with this she captured the heart of the nation and the world. Somewhere deep within, we are all capable of recognizing those feelings of love and loss.

When she turned to speak to the Vice President I thought, *I know that feeling. It's when you turn around and wonder, "Now what do I do?"* Your sense of direction and purpose has been altered. When the person you love has been taken by death, you just turn around and they are gone. It is an empty, hollow feeling.

That week's events triggered old memories from several areas of my life. All at once I was dealing with war, the death of a president, pictures of a flag-draped casket and a mourning widow, and my personal inability to hold down a real job that would allow me an identity and recognition for my work. It felt like it was the 1960's all over again.

As I sat at the computer in my bedroom, the words, "**It just does not matter**" entered my mind. Again, the words repeated in my brain: "**It just does not matter. The job at the paper really does not matter. Whether you are accepted or receive recognition from your work at the**

Finale

paper just does not matter."

The words felt surprisingly refreshing. I let them repeat over and over in my mind.

"What does matter, Glenda, is that in one brief moment you recognized, felt and understood that look Nancy Reagan had when she turned from the casket of her husband.

"What matters, Glenda, is that you recognized the feeling of the soldier who was wounded.

"You understand the inability to grasp the complexity of wounded emotions. It matters that you know that if he does not receive treatment for his emotional wounds as well as his physical ones, he will most likely live in the dark shadows of survival for a long time.

"That is what matters to you. That is what you are about and who you are. Anything other than what you are about just does not matter.

"In fact, should you be offered the greatest of opportunity tomorrow, you can offer it up, step back, and allow your coworker to have it, because it is not what you are about. And if it is not what you are about, it just does not matter."

My mind began to clear. I stopped struggling with trying to be accepted by a world that was not meant to be mine.

The next day, as I repeated the words to myself, my lips curved upward and peace flowed into my heart.

My workday was almost over when two curious looking men entered the office. As I walked by them I heard one say that they were from the Associated Press (AP). Baker City does not see many AP reporters and photographers.

Sacred Shadow, Sacred Ground

As I sit at my desk the thought crossed my mind, *Is there a big news story breaking for real?* I assured myself that if there was, I would be happy to just step aside and allow my coworker the honor. The thought brought a smile to my face.

The AP photographer carried a digital camera to drool over. I decided to strike up a conversation with him and for a while we talked about photo equipment. Then we talked about the photo opportunities of an AP photographer. He had just returned from California where he covered the Reagan story. Even though he had traveled world wide, he told me how he loved Oregon and couldn't wait to get back. We spoke of the countries he had visited and I asked him about his time in Washington, D.C. I told him about my journey to the Wall last November. I told him about the book I was writing, *A Vietnam War Widow's Journey Through Unresolved Grief*.

In those few moments, we traveled the world that led back to Enterprise, Oregon where Bruce is buried. I shared with him that Enterprise is a photographer's heaven.

When it was time for them to leave, he wished me well. "Good luck on the book," he said. "I'll watch for it, you're my hero." I had never heard those words directed at me before. I was shocked.

As I looked at this tall, well-traveled Black man in his bright yellow vest I said, "And you are my hero." I fought to keep the tears from surfacing. His words touched my heart.

That night I watched the intimate funeral service held in California for former President Reagan. The soldiers folded the flag with the same precision with which fellow

Finale

Marines had folded Bruce's. I watched in anticipation as they handed it to Nancy. My heart ached as she clutched it to her heart. For a moment, she represented every military widow in our country.

Her small, fragile body was filled with inner strength as she went to the casket. She was teaching me—along with our nation—how to say good-bye. She was strong enough to cry in front of the world for the one she so desperately loved. The torch has been passed to another generation. She has quietly given new widows of war permission to shed their tears.

That night I knelt and surrendered my struggling human nature. I asked for forgiveness for my frailties and humbly accepted God's will for the next part of my journey.

For days, I battled against finishing this quest while my conscious self wanted to playfully bask in the sun. I didn't understand the inner conflict.

As I calmed myself I heard, **"Are you ready? This will be the hardest thing you've done yet. Are you sure you are ready?"**

Okay God, You brought me this far. I am ready. I'm really ready to end this part of my journey. I don't know how anything can be harder than what I have already come through.

It felt like "Mission Impossible." I had a choice to make: I must consciously accept the mission of finishing my journey, or not. I had to acknowledge my faith because only a Power greater than myself could give me the strength to complete my climb to the top of Recovery Mountain.

"This is where the end meets the beginning and the

beginning meets the end. You must be ready to crawl, scrape, and fight through the last stretch. You will pull yourself to the top of the mountain over rough granite with hands scraped raw. You have to really want to get to the top." I felt the seriousness of the call as I accepted the challenge.

The next day on my way home, a deer walked out from behind the trees beside the small bridge a mile from my house. I stopped my car on the highway and looked into her big brown eyes as she stared back at me. When I reached for my camera she perked up as if startled. I spoke within my heart and assured the beautiful, gentle doe that I was not there to hurt her. She settled down and began to graze beside the road while I continued to watch and photograph her.

As I talked with a friend about the events of the week, it dawned on me that everything that happened was preparing me for my next step. "I'm getting ready for the funeral, the good-bye, aren't I?" I didn't write anything about Bruce's funeral service because I can't remember that part.

I hadn't allowed myself to think about the inevitable moment when I would have to say good-bye and walk away. He's been dead for 36 years and I still don't know how to say good-bye. How do I write words I don't know?

GOOD-BYE LETTERS

Sacred Shadow, Sacred Ground

1 August '68
"My Darling Wife,
Hello honey, I thought I would take this opportunity to let you know how I feel about a few things, mainly you.

Darling I want you to know that no matter what ever happens or how down and out things seem to be that you have brought me more happiness than I have ever known previously in my life.

You have made the difference in my life about which way to follow. Your faith and honest straight forward way of life has shown me how much life has to offer if I lead the right life.

I have happiness and trust in my fellow man, but most of all I have you and that means having a love so enormous that there are no words that can come close to describing the immensity of my love for you.

Now that our last few moments for being together for so long is coming around I realize just how fortunate I have been. Getting a woman like you has changed my life to the one that I needed so desperately to live and thanks to you darling I'm leading that life now. I'll be eternally grateful to God and you for showing me how much love means in my life. For without God and you I am nothing. Thank you darling. Thank you so very much."

With my eternal love
Bruce

Bruce leaving from Pendleton, Oregon. The last time I saw him.

Sacred Shadow, Sacred Ground

June 14, 2004
Cemetery, Enterprise, Oregon

Dear Bruce,

I'm sitting on the grass beside your grave. The breeze is blowing; there are clouds covering the tips of the mountains. It is quiet. The sun is shining its warmth on my skin. Flowers left over from Memorial Day spot the graveyard. I'm surprised by the number of ground squirrels scampering about.

I've tried to tell you good-bye so many times before. But this time it must come from the inner sanctuary of my heart. This time I have to separate myself from the shroud of sorrow as I walk away from your grave.

It is interesting to me that the beginning and end should meet on the same day and at a place we visited together 36 years ago. Today is the 36th anniversary of our wedding day and I am sitting along the same path we walked together so many years ago. This place has haunted me and at the same time comforted me many times as I've tried over and over to walk on by myself. My journey that brought me here today started when I said "I do" 36 years ago. I finally know that.

We didn't get to spend a lot of time together. Our whole life together took place within 6 months. You were a proud Marine when I met you. It comforts my heart to know that as much as you loved the Marines, you loved our life and was looking forward to the sharing of our future.

It comforts me also to know that within less than a month's time you were smart enough to see that the war in Vietnam did not make sense.

Good-Bye Letters

When you died, I not only lost you, I lost me. All the hopes and dreams for our lifetime together were snatched away in the blink of an eye. It changed my whole concept and understanding of life. While other people my age planned for their future, I had lost mine.

Future? There was no such thing. Forever was a very short time. Right or wrong, it was my reality.

I wish I could express myself more eloquently because today I want to finish saying whatever I need to say to you that will enable us to live freely in our own realm of life.

Thank you so much for helping me along my journey through my unresolved grief.

Every time I picked up your wrist watch and the second hand started dancing around its face, I knew you were with me. I knew because the watch didn't tick all the time. It seemed to only run when I needed confirmation that I was on course.

This journey has been long and hard. I buried your memory so deeply that I had to dive into the depth of my being to drag it out. As I excavated the sorrow, I had to feel it's pain and wash the wounds with my tears.

I can think of you now without the intense pain that used to accompany the mention of your name. I can share memories of you with people who also love you. You have a great nephew who loves to hear about you. Your sister calls him Brucie sometimes because he is so much like you. The rest of your family and friends also miss you, just as I do.

Today I am separating myself from the sadness. I actually feel closer to you than ever before.

Revisiting our life together has allowed me to know you and myself better. I can remember what it felt like to be 19. I can feel your presence and I wish we were just starting out again. I can remember the good and not just the pain of loss.

I felt like I failed you because I didn't go on living the way you wanted me to. But today I realize I did go on with my life. I survived. Because of my own struggle I have a better understanding of the words I placed on your tombstone. "For those who fight for it, life has a taste the protected will never know." I realize it was intended to be a Marine saying but I have fought for my life also. I have been a warrior in the emotional and spiritual part of my life and in that I know you would be proud because I managed to survive.

They say that when someone dies they leave you a gift. You left me the most precious gift of all. I will always know I was truly loved. You died in that magical time of our relationship when we had all the hopes and dreams of our future to look forward to. You died before we had to make the everyday compromises so many couples experience. I know I had clarity of mind and good judgment when I picked you. You really were trustworthy, kind, compassionate, sensitive, loyal, smart and strong. I loved your sense of humor and your boyhood charm. No one with their criticisms or unkind words can diminish this gift of love we shared. It is my eternal reality.

Thank you, my darling, for that most precious gift.

Without you I would not have traveled this road through my life journey. I would not be completing this written account of resolving my grief.

It is fitting that I am here today preparing to say another "I do." An "I do" to living my life.

The air is fresh. The breeze causes the trees to wave their limbs and the sun is still shining and the birds are still singing.

Good-Bye Letters

I could sit here for hours. It feels like an open living room.

My heart is peaceful and I feel like my inner compass has been repaired.

I know who I am. I know I am a good person and that I have a good heart. I am strong, kind, trustworthy, loving, and confident (on most days) and I look forward to new adventures. I don't feel lost anymore.

There is room for your memory to live within my heart. I have become who I am because of you. Thank you so much for coming into my life. Thank you for your love and commitment to God, to me and to our country. Your goodness will always be with me.

Leaving your grave scares me because I can still visualize the sadness hovering over the young girl leaving you at the cemetery 36 years ago. I don't know how this will be different.

I don't know how it will feel.

I want to leave knowing I've done a good job and that I have completed my work. That's kinda' like dying, isn't it?

When I drive down the hill, will I feel like I've left something behind and that I've left too soon?

Too soon? It's been 36 years.

Your body is underground, rotted away and soon mine will join you. But you are not in the grave.

I feel your adventurous spirit soaring over the mountain range. I feel you inviting me to come fly in a higher realm of living. All I am leaving behind is the sadness and sorrow.

My feelings are intact, my communication line with my higher power is open and my heart is peaceful. With the fresh wind of the spirit blowing on my face I know I am ready. I sit poised like a captive bird needing to be nudged from the familiarity of its cage.

Sacred Shadow, Sacred Ground

My inner voice said with the authority of a parent: **"You can choose to stay or you can choose to go, but you must choose, right now."**

My Eternal Love,
glinda

S.W.A.K.F.E.A.E.

AFTERWORD
"IT IS FINISHED"

Sacred Shadow, Sacred Ground

"I'm thinking about using a pen name for my book," I said, sitting in front of my therapist. "I realize with a story like this there will be a lot of criticism."

The few days before my appointment I had been dealing with people in my life who are very critical. People who seem to need to put someone else down to feel good about themselves. People who reminded me of my failures to make their successes seem more grand.

"I've written this from the very core of my heart," I continued, listing several reasons to justify why I thought it would be a good idea. "I enjoy my privacy."

I finished my good-bye letter. I no longer felt a need for recognition. We discussed the possibilities. I even considered the name of my grandmother, Sofia, as my pen name. "Pray about it," she said as I was getting ready to leave. "I know God will lead you to the right decision."

When I got home I sent an E-mail to a friend telling her I had decided to use a pen name. She didn't readily accept my decision and gave me other aspects to think about. The more I tried to explain it to her the more I had to think about the "real" reason and the benefits and drawbacks of using a different name. Bruce could use his name but I would change mine. No one could hurt him with their cutting, critical remarks. I was tired of fighting to be understood.

On the one hand I could remain anonymous and shirk my identity; on the other, I could accept the person I have become. I began to realize that by not using my name I would not be taking my place beside Bruce in the

Afterword

history of our life. I was trying to justify and allow myself to slip back into the shadows, away from the scrutiny of public opinion.

Painful events and criticisms were reasons I retreated years ago. I have finally found my way out and now I want to go back? Finding my voice has brought me nothing but an inability to be silent when I see an injustice.

I am opinionated. I show emotion. I refuse to be silenced by bullies and people who use intimidation.

When I realized using a pen name was a way for me to retreat I decided against it. I am not the same person. I am strong now. This is why I lived. This could be the accomplishment God would have shown me had I used that syringe in 1980.

It was storming outside. I made coffee and took my thoughts with me as I went to sit on my front porch to watch the lightning and hear the thunder. I decided I would keep my identity I had fought so hard to find. I would place my name boldly on the creation Bruce and I gave our life for.

It was a great storm. The rain came down and the thunder roared. As storms do, it began to pass.

I looked to my left as the sun came from behind the clouds before going down behind the mountain. It cast golden light through the large pine trees making shadows lay across the freshly cleansed ground. The light sparkled off the raindrops that lingered on the blades of grass. It was so beautiful tears began to flow down my face. I looked to my right. The sun highlighted the telephone pole and made it look like a cross. It stood with the dark stormy sky as its backdrop with two rainbows announcing

Sacred Shadow, Sacred Ground

God's promise. When the rainbows disappeared, I could see the storm traveling away from me as lightning flashed and hammered the earth reminding me of God's power.

I knew the war within myself was finished. I have accepted the gift of life.

"Good night, sweet prince."

Acknowledgments

I am eternally grateful to all of you who have given me encouragement, support and prayers throughout the process of writing this book. Not only have you helped me complete this project, you have helped me to heal from my unresolved grief. Many who have touched my life and my heart are not listed here. It is impossible to list the names of every person with whom I have come in contact. Each person and each interaction has made a difference.

Thank You:

To **God**: for supplying my needs, bringing me comfort, giving me strength and for synchronizing this miraculous journey of my life.

To **the family and friends of The Seven:** Francis, Roseann, Bob, Jim, James, Mary, Ed, Mr. and Mrs Evans, Edna and Colleen. Thank you for remembering and honoring the young men who died together on September 11, 1968 in Quang Nam Province, Vietnam. We share that one important moment in history when our lives changed forever. We are family.

To **members of Fox and Hotel companies, 2nd Battalion, 5th Marines:** Eugene, Dennis, J. D., Ken, Dave, Chris, James A., David B., Lawrence, Richard, Ron, Donald, Billy, Bill M., Steve, Robert S., Artie, Alfred, Dan, Roberto, Brad, Oren, Rod and Marc. You have helped me to understand the reality of war. Because of you, I know Bruce the Marine so much better. I am grateful for your loyalty to the memory of your fallen brothers and for accepting me as part of the family of Marines in which Bruce was so proud to belong.

To **Rosina Armon:** To Rosina for taking on the task of being one of my "front line" editors. Your encouragement along with your expertise in writing has helped this work become a reality. In the last fifteen years you have witnessed many of my life changes. It is good to have a friend with whom I can look back and say, "Remember when?"

To **Lisa Britton:** You selflessly served as my other "front line" editor. You have been a constant inspiration on this journey. Along with your many talents, you have a kind and gentle spirit. Through you I have been able to revisit the innocence of my youth that was lost so long ago. The loyalty of your friendship is a great gift and one I cherish. For me, you represent the goodness of humanity.

To **Chris Brown**—Also known as "The Locator": Chris is responsible for helping me find families of those who died with Bruce. He also helped me to locate the Marines who were at or near the Ambush site.

To **John and Betsy Campbell:** Thank you for meeting me and becoming a part of my first experience at the wall in November 2003. John is the author of *They Were Ours: Glucester County's Loss in Vietnam*. Fred Spina, included in his book was one of the Marines killed with Bruce. My visit to the Vietnam Memorial Wall in Washington, D. C.

was a very healing experience, thanks to both of you. John was one of the first to begin locating and connecting families. Along with his book, he helped with the research for the book *Shrapnel in the Heart*, by Laura Palmer.

To **Jim Carney:** Jim is the first of the family members I was able to contact. His friend Jerry Evans name is two lines below Bruce on the wall. Jim places a picture of Bruce and Jerry each time he visits the Vietnam Memorial in Washington, D.C. He and his girl friend Lee, accompanied me to the wall on my first visit in November 2003. I am grateful for the time we were able to spend together and for the many gestures of friendship you share.

To **Eugene Caster:** How do I thank you? You are truly a God-send. The divine intervention that we share is one of the most extraordinary events that has happened throughout this process. You stood on the sacred ground of my book in Vietnam over three decades ago and connected with me over 30 years later through a thing called the *Internet*. You provided me with a missing link to my broken emotional chain. You helped me to see beyond myself and realize that this book was about more than me. We cried and laughed together. You gave me courage and strength as I come out of the shadows into the light of my life. I am so grateful you answered the call that made you a messenger.

To **Shirley Chrisco:** My big "Siiister." Sisters share the most intimate details...and we have.

To **Edna Harwood** (mom): You lost the daughter you

knew, the one you hoped to have and many years of life experiences we could have shared. Thank you for your support and love you have given throughout my life.

To **Fumiko Hori** (My Sensei): You have been my guide from the beginning of this pilgrimage. Thank you for believing in me and allowing me to use your strength until I could find my own. Many times I stumbled but you never lost faith. You were committed to the process of healing, and understood the need for me to walk at my own pace. Your ability to be "real" while in your professional role as my therapist enlightened me. You know the tears I've shed, the fears I've felt, the challenges I've overcome. You know the personal dragons I have slain and you nurtured me while my wounds healed. Thank you for sharing your faith and for being you. I am eternally grateful.

To **Pauline Laurent** (Author of *Grief Denied A Vietnam Widow's Story*): You dared to travel this journey long before I began my own. You are strong, courageous and an inspiration to me. When I saw the picture of you at the wall, I knew I had to go there. I was just beginning my journey when I read your book. By being the first Vietnam war widow to publish your story, you let me know that completing my personal quest through unresolved grief could be attained. It made the road I was on a little easier to travel. When I began to doubt my ability to complete this horrific journey, you gave me hope. I read your words over and over until I could believe them and let them give me strength. When you said, "I have not done anything that you cannot do. It's all a matter of believing that you can," I listened. Thank you.

To **Timothy Lucas**: The graphic artist who willingly and selflessly took on the challenge of dealing with this very opinionated, decisive first-time author.

To **Diane Potter:** Thank you, Diane, for helping me to remember the details that I had buried so deeply. You have helped me to understand the reality of life after war and what it was like for many of the women whose husbands returned. You helped me to put my loss in perspective. I'm glad we reconnected and have the opportunity to share the truths of what happened to us after the war.

To **Susan Roberts:** Thank you, Susan, for the care that you and your daughters have given to Bruce's grave. Your loyalty and kindness have touched my heart.

To **Paul and Cyndy Stancliff**: Thank you so much for your volunteer service and for making it possible for me to reach my destination in Washington, D. C. The many services you provide help us to truly "come home."

To **Dana "Dusty" Shuster**, a poet who served as a nurse in Vietnam: We met in November 2003 while in Washington D. C. Thank you for sharing your story and for your words of wisdom. I am glad I got to hear you read from your work, *Battle Dressing: Poems about the Journey of a Nurse in Vietnam*.

To **Elenor Skarznski**, widow of Richard "Ski" Skarznski: The words you spoke to me by phone made a difference in my life. You helped me to understand the special gift Bruce left behind.

To my niece, **Lisa Steele:** Your loving spirit and all

those little extra things you did for me helped me to regain my strength.

To **Dylan and Zachary Steele:** You are the loves of my life. When you are older and read this book, I want you to know you helped me to live through this process, and gave me a reason to finish my work.

Dylan, I was privileged to be the one to comfort you through your first broken heart. I will always cherish the moment I held you while big tears ran down your face after you said good-bye to your dog, Chief. In your childhood innocence, you told me exactly what it felt like to lose the pet you loved. "It's like a bad dream, I just want to wake up and have it not be true."

Zachary, you believed me. As we walked to go visit Mr. Pine Tree, I told you we can commune with the trees and animals. You didn't see me smile as I watched your trusting child body hug the big pine. Later, you reminded me, "They can hear you when you talk to them from your heart." With that one sentence I rejoiced because I knew you "got it." I knew someone finally understood what I was trying to say. You were just seven. We three will make more memories and hug more trees.

To **Sharon and Larry Whitmire:** My first trip to Washington, D.C., was a major event. I had never flown commercially. Sharon was the one who guided me through the process of finding the airline, buying the ticket and getting on the plane. She understood my problem with anxiety. The night before my flight she and Larry took me to the airport for a practice run. She assured me most airports are set up similarly which probably kept me from having a serious panic attack.

To **Margaret Upton:** This is the result of what you started. Can your students learn to have compassion? Can they see the benefit of acceptance and respect? Will they take the time to be gentle and kind? These are the things that you gave to me over 14 years ago. These are the things that effectuate change. You were the angel that brought me to shore. Thank you for being you and for teaching me, *There Is No Such Place as Far Away.*

I could not have completed this life work if not for all the people who have touched my life. These few words do not do justice to the gratitude I feel in my heart.

Recommended Reading

Grief Denied: A Vietnam Widow's Story, by Pauline Laurent. *Grief Denied* is a strong read for anyone who has unresolved grief issues. It dips into the depth of despair and brings us out into the light of hope.

They Were Ours: Gloucester County's Loss In Vietnam, by John Campbell. Campbell found and interviewed family and friends of the 43 soldiers from Gloucester County, New Jersey, who were killed in Vietnam. These stories will touch your heart as you share in the lives of those who paid the ultimate price.

Shrapnel in the Heart: Letters and Remembrances from the Vietnam Veterans Memorial, by Laura Palmer. This book gives voice to families and friends of those who died in Vietnam. Take a glimpse into the hearts of everyday Americans who belong to the names on the wall.

Battle Dressing: Poems about the Journey of a Nurse in Vietnam, by Dana "Dusty" Shuster. Powerfully written poetry that gives insight to the compassion and strength of character of the nurses who served in Vietnam. Dusty tells it like it was and arouses the passion that comes from within the human spirit.

ABOUT THE AUTHOR

Raised in Milton-Freewater, Oregon, Glenda M. Carter continues to live at the foot of the beautiful Elkhorn Mountains in Northeastern Oregon. An accomplished fine arts photographer, Glenda intends on writing more books in the future.

Ordering Information

Regular retail price: $18.95

Bulk Orders: (25 or more), please contact publisher.

Shipping and Handling
Priority Mail: $4.50
Book Rate: First book: $3.85; additional books: $2.85 p/book. For orders over six (6), please contact publisher for shipping charges (subject to change).

To order: For mail orders, send payment (Money Order or Cashier's Check) for book(s) and S&H, payable to:
**Two Rainbows Publishing
P.O. Box 89
North Powder, OR 97867**

For **online** orders, go to:
www.tworainbowspublishing.com/order.htm/

*Please include your name and complete mailing address.